Relationship Blues

Relationship Blues

By

Joyce Payne

With drawings by Cindy Rhodes

www.relationshipblues.com

ISBN: 1-58721-731-7

1stBooks - rev. 9/8/00

About The Book

Relationship—clearly the most thoroughly discussed term in our contemporary lexicon—morphs into a tangible presence from a composite of all the real and imagined behavior we have assigned it. This story allows us to look through the Relationship's eyes at both sides of the gender gulf, as it ploughs through the middle—experiencing the disappointment, heartbreak, and hilarity, of our relentless trek, while attempting to retain a core of its own self.

Feeling rejected at being bounced from one couple to another, the Relationship executes a colorful and thought provoking romp through the confusing ritual that currently drives our exhausted engines of comprehension.

This Relationship is spunky—cunning—clever—clinging—obsessive—endearing—painful—vulnerable—destructive, and available. Love it or leave it, but you will never hear, or encounter the term relationship again without thinking of this special one. And oh yes, it wants to come and live with you.

To My Family

CONTENTS

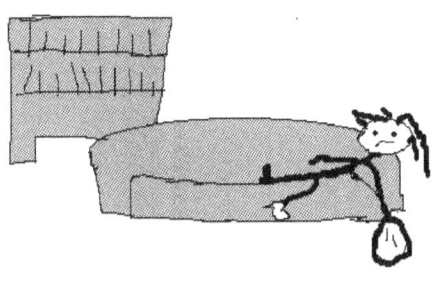

The Relationship Gets a Life

Saturdays were tough for Honey since Harold left. She wondered if she should have tried to talk him out of the temporary split—keep him close by, so they could work on the Relationship together. She was afraid that temporary might stretch into permanent and there would be no way of getting him back.

The Relationship sat in a corner of the plush, mauve, sofa facing the bookshelf and fireplace—in Honey's comfortable townhouse, its little legs stretched along the surface and crossed at the ankles. The tiny appendages were too short to hang over the edge and reach the floor where its always ready survival satchel was stashed for a quick get-away It sat alone, smirk in place, sweat shirt with an "R in front—running shoe on the left foot, stylish pump on the right—dark hair spiked straight up from the left side of its head, and long blond page boy scroll hanging from the other. The duality of the fashion statement revealed the paradox of its function, which currently seemed to focus on mediating the great modern hunger for connection and the inexplicable push to keep it away. Like super balls, glancing off one another—missing the all important "human moments"—the faint of heart and thick of head, painted themselves into their separate corners of loneliness. Even an attempt to rewire the general disconnect, was a tall order for the little creature, born of default, but savvy to the wiles of the ungracious.

So, it sat there scoping out the situation and gauging the options—agonizing over the ridiculous role it had no part in creating.   It felt trapped and slightly bitter—slowly drifting down to wallow in self-pity.   Thinking forward—thinking back—light and heavy—fighting the debilitating plague of humble beginingitis and incipient victimhood All this going through its head while Honey performed her Saturday morning frenzy-dip. Up, down, all around, puttering first in one room and then the other, finally settling on arranging and rearranging her acquisition of self-help books and magazines that had cover titles or lead articles with the word "Relationship" prominently displayed. The last book was titled, "How to Control Your Relationship." She placed that one on top.

The Relationship shrugged its shoulders, smirked, and mouthed the words, "It won't happen." On the plus side, it had to admit that the "R" word's popularity gave it name recognition and a certain degree of power. Still, it was not happy with its designated role of—moderator—insulator—hockey puck, for two people—like the offspring of a shared custody agreement—shuttled from place to place and left to negotiate its own priorities.

The Relationship thought the sappiness of it all, hung on a generation so busy doing their own thing—and being critiqued by the performance judges on every personal activity—they had become fearful of their own vulnerability and lost the ability to focus on anything outside the cocoon of the Me Zone. And the terminally endangered terms such as—love—faithful—forever—trust, and romance, had slipped out of their working vocabularies, due to a lack of requisite moral elbow grease to keep them active. The irony, the Relationship knew, was that those terms and accompanying feelings were the only things not being exercised as part of the current fitness craze.

And so, the Artful Dodgers, bobbing and weaving—tucking and rolling away from the tough stuff, began casting about for a less threatening—generic—expression, and finally fell like a ton of tofu on the versatile, one-size-fits-all, chameleon, "Relationship"—the cloying metaphor for, "Oh what a tangled web we weave." As the word flourished through endless repetition in print, conversations, and TV Talk Shows, the Relationship, now in the public domain, was born and given life.

Sinking back into the soft velvet upholstery of the sofa, the Relationship began to reflect on its predicament and felt a maudlin haze drop over its head. Thinking about its origins and creation due to benign neglect was not something to be proud of. It was tired of being treated like an incorrigible child., as the creators skillfully avoided the kind of care their product needed for a healthy life. These kinds of slights though, would have to wait until the appropriate time for revelation and paybacks. The Relationship had been around long enough to have learned from the offspring of the rich and famous how important it was to save things with which to even the score for real or imagined slights, neglect, and abuse, and had begun to keep a chit list for retribution if needed somewhere down the road. But at the moment it had a role to play—a destiny to fulfill—a life to live. It needed to sharpen its wit to keep from sinking into the widening chasm between Honey and Harold. The smart thing right now was to plan its own agenda, work on a game plan.

The little slug pinched a pill of lint from a cushion and blew the fuzz ball into the air. It needed time to think—about itself and the future. Honey and Harold would turn in one direction or another, but the Relationship didn't plan to hang around forever accommodating their trip. It had to focus on developing some kind of heart jerking story of how it overcame its humble beginnings—and sell it. The market was wide open. Humble and pathetic origins were where stars were born. Dirt poor was a badge of honor. Dirt of all kinds, even filth in your background was a kind of power all of its own, all kinds of disgusting behavior was fodder for fame, if you knew how to use it. Weird and quirky was even better. Things were being created every day with some sort of artificial engineering. If you came off the lid of a Skippy peanut butter jar, you could make all the TV Talk Shows for years to come. A power surge bolted through the Relationship's little body as dreams of having it all sucked on its brain. At the moment, though, the Honey and Harold deal was the only game in town. Patience was called for until the vehicle for the big breakthrough came along. An upwardly mobile couple without conscience would be perfect. The Relationship turned its attention back to Honey and her major problem, which was that all consuming missing piece of her life puzzle.

There had always been that same hole in the picture. She knew that Harold was the missing piece, and in his absent minded way, she suspected he had stashed himself somewhere and lost the exit directions. The Relationship thought the best part about Harold was when he went missing. Still, Honey was continually trying to find that errant cutout and force it into the empty place. Possibly that was what she was doing to Harold, forcing him to complete a picture he couldn't see himself in. The Relationship thought Harold's horse blinder, tunnel vision kept him from seeing the forest for the trees and the vision of the juicy morsel, Honey, for his fuzziness that hung in the air like a haze of confusion.

That was the incongruity of the situation—Honey was a complete confection, like freshly pulled taffy—her skin was all glistening and smooth and her face radiating her sunny disposition was surrounded with soft tawny colored hair, with light streaks in contrast to the dark, long eyelashes and warm brown eyes. And she was the epitome of a well rounded personality. She had large numbers of friends and admirers and a very successful career as a social worker, in which she made important decisions every day. In fact, she possessed the ability to focus an unwavering concentration and determination that could penetrate a wall of steel. But when it came to Harold, her concentration became a fixation—in fact an out of control roller coaster, that buzzed her brain into giddiness. The Relationship felt a pang of sympathy for Honey, as she placed her faith in the ritual of preparation that would surely bring Harold back.

She spread her hands across the surfaces of the table, chairs, sofa, and bookshelf, soothing the planes and anointing every object. When everything had been smoothed and patted, she tapped each article with the two middle fingers of her right hand—the gesture conveying her special grace. Tap, tap, there, there. Tap, tap. Not to worry. She tapped the Relationship on its head and then went to check the answering machine for the zillionth time. The Relationship thought she ought to tap, tap the top of her own head, since that's where the problem was.

Seemingly undaunted by the diminishing possibilities of Harold's return, Honey proceeded to the sanctuary of her kitchen, pulled the Relationship up on a high counter stool— removed the veggies du jour from the fridge and began the last rites ceremony.

Holding up the glistening eggplant with its sleek purple skin, bright green jester's topknot and graceful shape, Honey spoke from her heart, "Your perfection makes me believe in a higher power—one with great organizational skills and a management style to keep the ball bouncing. From planting the seeds, through the nurturing process and on to provide the next group with the strength and will to bring beauty and happiness to the world—and have some fun, too," said the chef with the heart of gold and a head full corn meal mush—getting down into a half baked culinary rendition of the twist—back and forth—see saw, see saw—wooden spoon in each hand and a jingle for the dance. "Do your knees hang low. Do they swivel to and fro? Do they scoot around the kitchen, for a Harold fixing mission?"   Do your knees hang low, can you tie them in a bow?" Rising from the crouch she rapped out the finale on the edge of the chopping block.

The Relationship covered its ears, to protect itself from a missionary in full throttle, but the people-to-plants message went on—coming close to an evangelist's priming of the congregation before asking for the weekly offering.

Honey delivered the sermon. "It's like this. Your clan has risen to the pinnacle of the food chain. You guys have been featured in gourmet magazines and exotic presentations in pricey restaurants," said the now swaying and chanting, food-chain-linker. "You have even spared your distant cousins of the field from becoming meat sauce, by substituting your own remarkable flesh to the diets of millions." Now, her voice low and convincing, threw in the hooker "So here's the deal. I seriously need to enlist your incomparable services for a very special project."

The Relationship twisted back and forth on the stool, playing a miniature game of soccer on the counter top by flicking a confused pea back and forth between two pods.

"You have it within your power to make the world a better place for all creatures large and small," said Honey, speaking now as the Health Food Guru to the raw recruits. If there had been a Humane Society for the Prevention of Cruelty to Veggies, She would have been the troop leader. "The problem is that my Relationship is going south, sour, kaput, down the tubes. Harold is flaking out on me. I know he is too serious and worries a lot about injustices in our world, but lately he has been showing signs of increasingly erratic behavior. I think he has a nutritional imbalance. He eats grunge food—stuff that's probably contaminated. So my wonderful little possessors of incredibly powerful vitamins for victory, this is where you come in," said Honey once more pressing the smooth skinned eggplant against her cheek. Then placing it on the counter, with an assortment of other produce, began the anointment process of transforming the vegetables into an enriching experience that would guide Harold to the high energy level he needed to "fix the world," while allowing the participating audience to see the value of their sacrifice.

"Trust me," said Honey, "Harold will elevate us all to heights we shall each be proud of, if only he has the strength to complete his mission." Then she placed a small china dish of leftover,   Rich and Famous Waldorf salad, topped with Debutante Chantilly Lace Dressing, in front of the Relationship—after slipping a paper doily underneath—"because they go together." It was Honey's belief that all things have a partner. Something or someone to belong to—two by two, that is the way it should be—Jack and Jill—Mom and Dad—peanut butter and jelly—Honey and Harold—that is the way it must be, if people are going to avoid the expanding loneliness in our culture. Honey remembered when Mother Teresa, the sainted nun, had visited the U.S. and remarked that the greatest sadness she observed was our overwhelming loneliness. This message inspired Honey to devise a personal numbers game, of two by two's, that she would play to correct the problem, if possible.

Back on the cutting board, Honey explained the procedure to the volunteers, who began to take on a certain willingness to shore up the flagging Harold. With the wooden spoon she tapped a tomato and an onion and said "You two go perfectly together. Always have, always will. Right?—Double your pleasure, double your fun," thwack, splat, thwack splat—"Double your bubbles until you are done." Sang the jingle happy cooker. "Think of yourselves as little missionaries," she said, dropping the vegetables in the pot and repeating the sequence until the counter was cleared. The Relationship thought after this latest pronouncement, that anyone sharing a plate of vegetables with Honey, would pause before digging into the martyrs and feeling like a cannibal. And besides, it felt the gang of power pulp had been too willing to walk the plank for human posterity. That maybe the veggies should have protested—attempted to negotiate—held out for some concessions, like more fertile soil and environmentally friendly fields, in which to prosper—kinder and gentler handling—beauty contests and higher prices at the Farmer's Markets—an extended shelf life.

The Relationship popped the tired pea in its mouth and quaked at how quickly it had fallen into Honey's grand scheme for Harold's enrichment program—even contemplating its role as arbiter for a better contract on behalf of the vegetables, was scary. The woman's power of mesmerizing was unique, possibly even dangerous, if she ever fell into evil hands. "And that concludes the entertainment part of the program," said Honey, tapping the wooden spoon against the now simmering pot. When there was nothing left to stir, pat, smooth or tap, the Relationship knew the metamorphoses from sane, capable person to hysterical nut cake was about to take place. Honey could no longer hold off the yearning—the compelling forces of addiction that permeated every part of her being and broke her resolve. The Harold suction was beginning to pull at her wavering control center.

Honey picked up the phone, shook it, blew into it, and heard only the dial tone. She looked once more at the non-blinking message recorder and pressed the button. Nothing. She pulled back the drapes in the front room window to survey the street and driveway—opened the door and pressed the door bell. The street and driveway showed no signs of a staggering, wounded, incoherent, figure (that would be Harold on his best day) that special person, who, in Honey's wildest dream sequence, might possibly have been overcome by fumes or shot in the head as he returned with love in his heart and the "M" word on his lips—while the faithless door chimes tinkled an empty tune. Drat! Still, the Relationship thought you could hardly help love someone, who rang the doorbell and answered it herself. Panic palpitations began to pound in Honey's chest forcing the blood to her face. Her one conscious thought: Where was Harold and at what point had the Relationship become a threat to him?

The Relationship watched as Honey's anxiety elements, turned on high, began to frazzle the protective coating and shut off the reasoning power to her brain. The Relationship began to miss Harold. At least he had provided a control valve in this nutsy network. It also knew that at any moment, Honey would make the inevitable call for help to her always available friend, Madge, whose record of failed relationships would probably fit in the Guinness Book. Oh well, it would do what it had to do while it planned for the future. Honey was ready to run and grab at whatever floating buoy Madge had to offer.

Three for Lunch—On the Rocks

The Relationship was dragging its feet—its little body leaning back, in a dead weight, protester's mode, against the jerking and pulling being applied to its right arm by the nearly hysterical Honey, as she made a frantic dash across the driveway and into the car. The Relationship hunkered down in the car seat. It was embarrassed and annoyed and it definitely did not want to "do" lunch again with Honey and her terminally boring friend, Madge, whose idea of support was to blow cliches in the air like a stream of soap bubbles through a plastic ring, and carrying about as much ballast. The Relationship blew a major spit bubble and let it slide down its chin.

Honey barreled through the doors of the entrance foyer of the up-scale restaurant with the Relationship in tow—her head bent—hair flying in her single-minded drive to dump her box of rocks on friend Madge. Oblivious to the Gaper's Block her entrance created, the true friends performed the ritual cheek to cheek kissies. The Relationship grimaced and ducked under a fold of table linen hanging from a nearby banquette.

"Honey, come here and sit down. You look absolutely frazzled," said Madge, clamping her caring clutch on Honey's shoulder and steering her, like a helpless drunk toward a private table. "I see what you're saying. I know what you're feeling. I can relate to that," said Madge, her motor mouth skipping the preliminaries and shifting into high gear.

"I haven't said anything yet, so how could you know what I'm feeling? And don't you mean hear what I'm saying?" said Honey with a sudden clue to the reality that her friend was a leaky vessel incapable of holding and assimilating the simplest piece of information.

The Relationship was struck with how quickly Madge's insipid talk- talk had brought Honey down from her mountain high, manic.

"Hey, its just TV empathy cant. Everybody says stuff like that. It's a way to make friends. If you feel their pain, you can bond with them," said Madge, pushing the envelope of credulity to the edge of the table.

14

"You want to bond with my pain?" asked Honey. "That's weird, Madge, I'm not comfortable with that stuff. I don't have that kind of pain, whatever it is.

"Yeah, right. So what's happened?"

"It's my Relationship," said Honey, falling into a chair— the torque from Madge's over- control— forcing her to sling the Relationship onto the vacant seat next to her, causing its head to strike the brass nail heads binding the leather chair. Drat! How it hated this public display of private affairs. The woman was out of control. She was becoming a menace to those around her. The Relationship pulled itself up, dipped one end of its napkin in a goblet of ice water and applied the cloth to the growing welt.

"Honey, I'm so sorry. I know what you're going through," said Madge, her empathy cant still directing the show. "Do you want to talk about it?"

"Well, I guess," said Honey, realizing that Madge's attention span had already had its single moment of exposure, but still needing to speak the painful words pressing against her heart. "It's my Relationship, it's in real trouble. I simply don't know how to deal with it anymore. I'm at my wits end."

The Relationship slumped back in its chair and smirked at the irony of the situation. It knew she had no wit left and there would be no end to anything, especially this nauseating conversation.

"You know, Madge, I've tried practically everything to improve my Relationship, but nothing seems to be working. I've been sensitive and caring. I've been tough and independent. I've been supportive, yet allowed it space. The bottom line is, the Relationship is running my life instead of the other way around and I don't know what more I can do to fix it," said the worry worn Honey, digging into her bag of limited nuggets. The Relationship felt itself lapsing into self pity. Its head was throbbing and it didn't want to listen to anymore bilge about its personal condition, but it knew the only escape from this mess was to tune out, or better yet, focus on the future. Sinking further into the chair, it began to pluck at the buttons on the leather upholstery.

"In fact," said Honey, "The truth is, and this may sound silly, (no kidding), but one of the problems with my Relationship is that it has lost its spontaneity. It has no sparkle—no fizz—no pop. It's practically dead in the water."

The Relationship put its finger sideways inside its mouth — created a vacuum and then forced the finger out, making a small pop.

"Well," said Madge, "these are very trying times and it's not easy to keep a Relationship afloat."

The Relationship pinched its little nose to indicate it was ready to hit the water in case the call for ditching was sounded. "Actually, Madge, I know that Harold loves me and I love him.

It's just that he isn't comfortable with this century—it doesn't work for him. It causes him to have a lot of hang-outs."

"Don't you mean Hang-ups?" suggested Madge.

"No, he never hangs up. He just goes to these places that remind him of the past and hangs out there. That's how he tries to deal with the present. It's like having his own personal time machine that he drives in reverse. He doesn't understand the Relationship. He doesn't see why there has to be some interpreter stuck between us. He finds it threatening. It's the Relationship that's the problem. It's very complex." Hearing this tidbit of sanity thrown into the hopper, the Relationship perked up. It stuck out its chin, rested its elbows on the chair arms and matched its fingertips. Then, interlocking all but the first two made a church and steeple without any people. It was a pose it liked to strike when affecting a posture of control. It was pleased to be called complex. It thought of itself as deep and intellectually superior in that context. Having gained back its waning confidence, the Relationship placed its thumbs in its ears, waggled its fingers and blew a raspberry at the world in general and the twits at the table in particular.

"You know something?" said Madge, "Maybe you ought to insist on a commitment. If your Relationship is running your life, it probably needs some restraints put on it. A forced commitment can often be the turning point for a Relationship."

17

A frightening picture flashed before the Relationship's eyes. It saw itself sitting alone on a bench, in a large room with bars on the windows, wearing a little white cotton jacket with wrap around sleeves tied in the back.

The Relationship hated that "C" word. Commitment had become a pox on free spirits and free association. Something needed to be done quickly to thwart the switch in direction this twiddle-twaddle had taken. Diversionary tactics were called for immediately. The Relationship reached across the table and fished a noodle out of Madge's side dish of pasta primavera— put one end between its lips and rapidly sucked in the long strand 'til the end of it flapped, splattering marinara sauce all over the white Battenburg place mats and crystal goblets. Then it pressed its finger on a pat of butter and wrote a dirty word on the shiny surface of the table. The rout was a dud. The talking heads pattered on without breaking stride.

"There is just one other thing you might want to consider," said Madge. "If your Relationship is so painful and difficult to deal with, maybe you ought to give up on it. I mean, if you have tried everything and it still isn't working out, why not just dump it? You can always get a new Relationship. Possibly one that would be easier to live with."

With that shot in the head, the Relationship pulled itself upright. If this gig didn't work out and it got replaced, the fun and games would be over. No more outings—no more lunches for playing the role of control freak. No more riding on the surface waiting for the "big one."

It blanched. It wanted to pick its own time to jump ship—when a rescue team was on the way. Was there still time to run in a survival play? It was worth a shot. Perhaps a warm smile would do it, or a genial manner, even a small hug. The scam would take practice, but—what was that Honey was saying? "I don't know, Madge, I've thought about that too, but I have put so much time and effort into this Relationship that I really hate to let it go."

The Relationship slacked back. Whew! It was still in the catbird seat. Not to worry, this savior of lost causes probably would not turn off the search lights until Harold was found and led to the safety of her care.

"Well then, as a last resort, why don't you take a break. Give your Relationship a rest. There's nothing like a vacation away from it all, to clear the air and get a different perspective," said Madge. The Relationship allowed as how the air definitely could use some clearing up, and a trip away from these dismal digs would be invigorating, revitalizing, and, if Honey would get off its case, just possibly a whole bunch of fun. "You're absolutely right, Madge. My Relationship definitely needs a rest. I'm going home and make reservations for a lovely quiet, resortful vacation. Sand and sea—reflecting—resting. That's the ticket," said Honey.

"You promise that you will let your Relationship take a break? That you will relax and think about something else?"

"I promise, Madge, I really do. I'm not going to give it a single thought. Thank you for your input. You are a real pal."

Its feet trailing behind---leaving tiny
little toe tracks in the sand

R & R & R & Honey

On the plane to the islands, the Relationship, seated next to Honey, had feelings of ambivalence. Maybe they could relax. Maybe she would stop her herky-jerky pursuit of Harold, but minutes into the air, Honey pulled out a book entitled "Tough Squeeze." She read for a while, then put the book down and gazed out the window. The pen she had been using to underline important passages was now pressed into the dimple in her cheek. She was contemplating the deeper meaning of the words as they may effect the Relationship. The Relationship suspected that some enterprising spirit must have lifted sections of recent best sellers on the Advice—How To list—cut them into strips horizontally—scrambled them together—tossed them in a spin dryer for a couple of cycles—hauled them out and randomly pasted the lines on paper.

With a catchy title such as, "Tough Squeeze," it couldn't miss. Hundreds of thousands of Honeys would rush out and claim the garbled message as the latest toe hold in Relationship Therapy. The Relationship felt stressed and strained. Honey had already broken her promise to Madge which was predicable, but disappointing. It wondered about the power of the written word; how much gobble de gook found its way into the mass market to give quasi hope to these floating water lilies. The Relationship began to feel sorry for Honey. She wasn't a bad sort. In fact it couldn't help liking her. She suited her name perfectly. She was incredibly sweet and her tawny colored hair and satin smooth skin gave an elastic grace to her movements. She was a confection...and hopelessly sticky when it came to Harold. Still, that was no reason to give in to her spasmodic dependency. Getting all simpy would spoil the fun and there was precious little fun to be had. The Relationship was afraid of taking on Honey's characteristics and losing its own perspective—its own special goal—the drive to Talk Show Valhalla.

Arriving, on the Island, the Relationship felt a deep depression coming on. It hoped the sea and sand vacation would clear these muddy waters, or at least block out their view. The

Relationship saw a glimmer of hope as it followed Honey—perky in her bright orange bikini—blond hair doing its what-the-hey bounce—stride almost confidently toward the row of lounge chairs lined up facing the sparkling water. But there the image dissolved, as she paused in front of the chairs, pen in hand, and silently began the one selection process she hoped would bring the magic of Harold into her aura. She circled each chair and tapped the back with her pen, then waved some invisible spirits to be seated. Finally assuming that one of them had settled in and might just be an incarnation of Harold's lap, she snuggled into the green and white striped beach chair. The Relationship paled and dove behind the chairs—too embarrassed to be part of this scene of arrested development.

Satisfied with her pick, Honey settled down and with conditioned response brought forth her current security blanket—the copy of "Tough Squeeze~ and propped it up in front of her for all the world to see. In minutes, the magnetic title of the B.S. (Best Seller) sucked up a woman five chairs away and deposited her in the empty one next to Honey. Strangely winded from such an easy jaunt, the woman panted out, "Hi, is this seat taken? I read that book last week. How do you like it? Do you find it helpful? I'm married."

"No, I'm not saving that seat," said Honey, "I'm here alone to do some serious thinking and to give my Relationship a long needed rest."

"Yes," I understand what you're saying. You are very wise to decide whether or not your Relationship is healthy enough to sustain a long commitment. Even a Committed Relationship can have problems," said the Married Stranger easing back into her chair and stretching out her legs. "Believe me, I know." The Relationship groaned and lolled its head from side to side. There was that stupid "C" word again, pitched by a surrogate Madge with the same mouth except for the air hissing out of it between questions. The Relationship, knowing it couldn't stomach another round of recycled diddly squat, got up from behind the chairs and shuffled twenty paces toward the edge of the water where a near mirror image of itself sat on a beach towel making drip castles from a bucket filled with sand and water. The little creature seemed to be wheezing.

"Excuse me, are you with her?" asked the Relationship inclining its head toward the woman seated next to Honey. "Yeah," said the little builder, "And him," it added, jerkinga sandy thumb in the direction of a male contortionist doing weird things with an exercise strap.

"What's your status?" asked the Relationship.

"Married, but in trouble" said the Married Relationship leaking air from its little nose like a deflating balloon. "Are you O.K.?" asked the Relationship. "I mean, there seems to be some trouble with your breathing."

"Yeah, I know." answered the Married Relationship, a bunch of air belching its way through the curled lips. "It comes with the territory."

"Well, what is it? Are you sick or something?"

"Sort of, but not really. I'm a victim of abuse."

"Geez, what kind? I don't see any lumps or bruises. Do they do it with rubber hoses?"

"No," said the pathetic little Married Relationship, releasing just the teensiest breeze from between its front teeth. "It's a respiratory battle—they fight with lung power."

"You mean they holler and scream at each other? Fling cutting remarks in their faces? Slam hateful accusations down their throats? Verbally grind down on their weak spots? That can sometimes lead to internal injuries of the head," said the Relationship, assuming a new mini role of counselor.

"No, no," said the Married Relationship. "They don't say anything—not one single word. They punch each other out with air. It's called sigh abuse."

"Wow, this is terrific. I've never heard of it before," said the Relationship, plumbing for humor in someone else's Heartbreak Hotel. But thought the word abuse had been slapped around so much it had lost its teeth. "It's not funny, in fact it's very dangerous living in a house where two Olympic class wind-blowers duke it out every day. I'm totally exhausted from bobbing and weaving, just to keep out of the cross current. If you had to live in a vortex of sigh abuse, you would be laughing out of the other side of your mouth—probably because you would have been smacked up side the head with a whooshing upper-cut," said the Married Relationship shooting a mean stream of air through its nostrils.

"Geez, I'm sorry, but it's pretty amusing on the face of it, and I'm really interested in how this old 'what for' gets started," said the Relationship, enthralled with this innovative method of destruction.

"O.K., it goes like this. The abuse is delivered through the cruelly directed release of air," said the Married Relationship, a small whisper of a breeze creeping from the corner of its mouth. "That woman up there has been pummeled, punched, and petrified, over a period of years, by that bag of gusting bellicosity over there," said the Married Relationship, pointing once more at the whirling warriors. "It's a very demeaning method. He has a round-house sigh that makes you know your life isn't worth a plug nickel. He sighs at her unmercifully all over the house. He even sighs at her in front of the children and when friends come to visit. It is very humiliating. I mean sometimes she would be just saying this or that, or laughing and he would smash her in the kisser with a sigh that had the velocity of a tornado as it swished through his teeth and vibrated his lips. He is a brute, but she is no slouch either. I've seen her blast away with some major jaw slackening sighs in his direction."

"I'm truly sorry that you have to live in this arena of windcuffs, but you ought to think seriously about your own breath control. You seem to have inherited a sigh gene compounded by learned behavior. It's a heck of a weapon."

Just as the Married Relationship began to stockpile large amounts of air for what looked like a major offensive, possibly aimed at the now wary Relationship, Honey sprinted over. The Relationship sagged as it saw that old glint of self determination in her eye and knew that she had probably overdosed on "Tough Squeeze˜ sauce laced with fortifying shots of hot air from the Married Stranger.

Honey jerked the Relationship off the beach towel by its arm and began dragging it like a rag doll across the beach toward the hotel room—its feet trailing behind— leaving tiny little toe tracks in the sand. Even in transit the Relationship knew she was about to make the inevitable phone call to Him. During the phone conversation, He—Harold agreed to work on the Relationship—to take more responsibility for it.

Row Yourself Cruise Ship

Eating Boxes With Harold

After the transfer "back home" to Harold's living quarters—existing quarters, the Relationship was tired and uncomfortable. The couch where it slept was full of potato chip crumbs and other cruddy leftovers. It hadn't felt well in these environs. It was afraid of the mire that collected in the refrigerator—especially the cloudy matter and saline crust that held the stagnant olives captive in the five opened jars and even worse, the green caterpillar fuzz that grew on the cheese. Harold just flicked it off with his thumb and forefinger and wolfed down the cheese. The Relationship was tired, too, of eating out of cardboard boxes and paper cartons with days old carry-out meals stuck to the sides.

Harold was talking on the phone which was tucked under his chin. His right hand holding the remote control device was flicking through the line up of selections. His left hand held the inevitable box of food, but he lacked an extra appendage to deliver the food to his mouth. The Relationship thought that the only thing that would improve Harold's way of life was if he had three hands—one grafted to the TV remote—one for lifting the food to his mouth and one sort of a free lance extension. What was puzzling, though, was that he never watched an entire program. He just clicked and clicked, as if the answer to the puzzle of his life would mysteriously appear on the screen. The Relationship knew that it was Honey on the other end of the line and assumed she had been dipping into the "Tough Squeeze" sauce again and was serving Harold with a final ultimatum. Shape Up, or Ship Out. In other words, the commitment proceedings had begun. Harold stared at the Relationship as it sat in its "apartment-power-position"—feet up on the coffee table— smirk in place and picking its teeth with the end of a long fireplace match.

"Yeah," he said, "I found the spinach soufflé in the fridge. I meant to call and thank you. Three kinds of cheese huh? Wow, I could tell it was special." The truth was, Harold had not even tasted the soufflé. It had gotten pushed back in the fathomless murk where it would not be touched until it grew hair.

"You bet, kiddo," he said. "I'm dealing with the big "R" right now. In fact I'm going up to the cottage this weekend to think things out—you know, get my head straight. O.K., talk to you later." That was it, Harold could never bring himself to end a call with, "I love you," even though the words were pulsating to get out.

The Relationship sat in the front seat of the car for the three hour drive up to the lake cottage, its feet propped up on the dashboard, and watched Harold's facial machinations as he worked on the puzzle that his life had become to him. He wished that he and Honey had been allowed more time together before they had gotten involved with the Relationship—before it was always there between them making demands and forcing them apart. The word itself carried too much heavy baggage— too many tales of woe, real or imagined, or retold from others— too many warning labels, and too many preconceived rules and regulations that boxed up the future and put a lid on it.

When Honey and Harold had met during his advertising days, their love affair was instant, pure and uncomplicated. She was a social worker and enjoyed the relative lightness of his advertising compared to the heaviness of her daily encounters with hardship. Honey was not absorbed with this kind of work. She was able to separate herself from the sadness—exult in the

31

progress—even to maintain a sense of humor, and eventually create make believe advertising copy as connecting love notes between herself and Harold. "Put a little sugar in your heart. Cover it with mincemeat for a tart. Take a bite today and love is on its way. So put a little sugar in your heart." Through Honey, Harold discovered the disparate avenues many lives took that ended in helplessness—dislocation and sometimes abuse of children. It was this concern for the children that became an obsession with Harold, along with many other quirky concerns that had moved in to play havoc with his balancing mechanism. The list was endless.

Harold was embarrassed by cults—buzzwords—slogans—designer emblems and contrived lingo that defined and protected "in-groups"—excluded all others and trivialized the high points of his life. He wondered why, once comfortable words he had worked and played with had become estranged—turned around and came back in a different guise, with an accent of meanness. Like the formerly respected word, commitment, now a one-sided threat to someone else's freedom of association. And other similarly redefined phrases that placed a pox on important, individual and personal experiences with names that no longer conjured up pleasant memories, but currently stuck to the masses like Velcro.

The Relationship wondered why Harold didn't step up to the problem and take a couple of whacks at it instead of hunkering down and mumbling to himself. It thought that Harold was too much of a Clark Kent, but that he had the qualities to be Superman if only he had the right costume. Then again, it knew that Harold would probably be most comfortable just hanging out in the telephone booth, and the costume was definitely out.

The Relationship knew that Harold didn't go to Health Clubs because he thought that dressing up in uniform exercise garb was superficial—and pumping on name-brand equipment for the purpose of over developing musculature for show and tell and passing it off as masculinity was embarrassing.

When he saw people parading their deltoids in shirts ringed under the arms and V shaped down the front in matching sweat patterns, he wondered if someone had begun to market an odorless sweat spray that could be applied to a garment to replicate that perfect work out sweat design. Or perhaps an even more avant-garde entrepreneur was already on the scene with permanently pre-stained shirts—in a kind of body fluid Rorschach—for the guy who didn't have the time or inclination to put forth all that effort, but would like to show visible signs of work out glamour juice. This kind of thinking, he knew, separated him from the inner circle of male bonding. Harold had a very low guyness quotient. Still, he couldn't help but wonder if all the energy by the pumping and rowing taking place in Health Clubs all over the world could be captured and put to use, that it might provide enough electrical power to fuel an entire city or a large ocean going vessel. He also wondered if, in ancient times, the prisoners who manned the oars on the slave ships—the crewmen bending into the heavy life-sucking task— their ankles shackled to the floor—subsisting on a meager diet of grains and rice—similar to the currently popular complex carbohydrate diet revered by exercise/fitness gurus—had at least, if nothing else, been proud of their muscles and in touch with their bodies. Harold was aware that this kind of thinking was bringing him precariously close to tipping over his own canoe. And the only person he could share these unbalancing thoughts with was Honey. She found them interesting—amusing, and not particularly threatening. She even wrote an advertising jingle featuring Harold's imagined sweat shirts. It read:

Tee Shape Sweats/Sweat Shape Tees—SWEAT-TEES Let Your Underarm Rings and Chest Sweat V's Make a Fashion Statement for You. Buy SWEAT-TEES the Pre-Stained Shirt for Hunks. The Perfect Pit Out Pattern for Popularity.

The Relationship thought the sweat shirt idea had merit, but that there was an even greater marketing potential in the "buff boys" at the rowing machines. **A Row Yourself Slave Ship Cruise** would be perfect for the guys who would like to combine

34

a Paradise Island Vacation with a Full Fitness Program. The advertising copy would read:

Yo, Ye Olde Crewmen. Not pulling your own weight? Bored with the Same Old, Same Old, Workout Routine? Disappointed in the over stated Endorphin High? Thrill gone from the Shackles, Chains, and Whips?

Have we got a trip for you!!!

Our Row Yourself Slave Ship Cruise Features
Old Fashioned—Exquisite Punishment
Penetrating Lashings for Permanent Show-Off Scars
One Oar to Each Guest—Wrists Appropriately Chained with Highest Quality Metal Manacles
Ankles Similarly Confined and Attached to the Floor for Maximum Pain While Stretching.
Abrasions and Scars to Impress Your Elitist Friends— Who Won't be Able to Say, "Been There, Done That."

For the Ultimate Living-on-the-Edge Experience

Half-Starved Rats—Trained for Combat—Will Scamper around in the Hold— Daring the Guests to Spar for the Dwindling Supply of Nutrients.

These Mental Calisthenics Designed to Outwit the Mischievous Rodents are Included at No Extra Cost—Due to the Occasional Loss of Guests, in this Category.

Bidding will Begin on Seat Assignments and Choice of Slave or Flogger Positions when Making Reservations.

The Relationship had to admit it had learned a lot from Honey and Harold that would give it a leg up when it split from them and could only imagine the lessons in ruthlessness it would learn from the couple without conscience. Still, it was growing weary of Harold's flakiness. It wished that he would spend more time hanging out in the parking lot of his apartment complex— talking guy talk with regular people about cars— boats—sports, or international affairs, instead of concerning himself with these obscure mental rituals. Or, if he had to dwell on the sappy side of life, at least do something about the world's dysfunction—get off the dime—lean into the turn. Better yet, write what was selling. He could make a lot of money out of smarm and degradation. It was popular stuff right now—boffo material— big bucks babies. It was time for Harold to give up his weird resistance to changing values—segue into contemporary life and accept the creed of greed.

Seeking Sanctuary at the Lake

In the car, Harold began processing air in and out between his teeth. He pounded on the steering wheel with the palms of his hands. He let out a low mournful wail and said, "Damn, damn, damn." The Relationship pulled its feet down—sat up straight and fastened its seat belt—an involuntary giggle escaped from its lips drawing a sappy glare from Harold. It knew that this was the part of the routine where Harold beat himself up because of his quasi non-conformist attitudes. He seemed to himself out of step and unable to click to someone else's clack and his sometimes uncontrollable zest for life and especially space for dreams to play—caught him with his directional signals blinking alternately and wildly out of sync.

Harold felt like a walking scoreboard where everything in his life flashed on a large screen indicating his level of performance as judged by contemporary cultural flacks. He felt even more concern for Honey, whose natural inclination to give her heart freely, had begun to pull back as the voices of the gender bender's conflicting rhetoric began to assert mental and emotional restraining straps on her innocent spontaneity.

Harold despised the whole banality of the battle of the sexes. Surely they were both worth preserving in some kind of harmony instead of the crippling sniping carried on between the two armed camps. He wished for a place where men and women could love wholeheartedly without an audience or a scorekeeper—without Relationships, or commitment creeps throwing their weight around. Damn that Relationship. Damn that "C" word. Damn the crummy society that put its big, fat foot on his throat.

Harold wondered if he accepted the commitment deal, he would be held down and given buzz speak drugs so that everything he said would come out as acceptable and he wouldn't care anymore about private and creative meandering.. Perhaps it would be a kind of brain laundering in which his spirit would be soaked in vats of cumulative triteness until it drowned. Or possibly, he could feign some kind of verbal compliance as a cover, and on certain days, away from the babble bunch, let his random thoughts out to play. Harold thought that people talked too much—talked everything to death—polluted the air with unnecessary and often cruel verbiage—the most injurious to the human spirit.

When he was in his advertising job, he designed an ad campaign for a Breath Mint. The story was titled, Twenty-four Hours of Silence, and portrayed people shouting, scolding, and generally mucking up someone else's life. In the opening segment of the commercial, people are gazing upward, their faces reflect a mean spirited, disgruntled demeanor. The sky is murky from an accumulation of thoughtless, even filthy remarks spewed into the atmosphere from mouths that needed cleansing and minds given time to think before further fouling the air.

As the pall thickens, and the words can no longer be heard, the mouths close in frustration, creating the Twenty Four Hours of Silence. The zipped lip gathering miraculously becomes aware that because of their self containment—nobody loses his job—no one's heart is broken, and no one suffers gross mouth humiliation. At the end of the time frame, the characters also notice that the fog has cleared due to their silence. People everywhere are smiling as they pop the green and white breath mints into their former orifices of pollution and exclaim, "Freshen your mouth and sweeten your words with Breath Kleen and make the world a better place in which to live."

Harold's TV commercial was considered the Bloopie of its time—laughed at— dumped on—ridiculed—recalled and pulled off the air after appearing only five times. The Breath Mint sponsor dumped the ad agency—the ad agency dumped Harold, but way too soon, as it turned out, because the substance of the commercial went on to star in a life of its own.

Late night comedians began to mimic the mint popping ad using their own scripts. Some of the "take offs" were hilarious. As the joke was passed around, it became common practice, when confronted by an offensive mouth polluter, to point to the sky and offer a breath mint. Harold had achieved the ultimate advertising goal—product identification for an entire industry. In the midst of all the notoriety, Harold declined interviews and job offers, blocking his 15 minutes of fame. Instead he hunkered down, hid out, and began to focus on his path of collecting the forces necessary to torque the world in a different direction. .

In the years previous to his advertising gambit, Harold wrote a series of children's books featuring families of mice in various countries around the world. Carefully researched, the stories depicted a kind of gentleness and ease through the pure and simple daily habits, interactions, celebrations, food and surroundings of a mother and father mouse and their young children, living in each of the countries featured. When. Harold traveled to foreign lands, he paid special attention to the antics, capers, games and silly behavior that—caused children to smile—how creative and spontaneous they were in making dull, ordinary, sad, and even threatening events into moments of hilarity. He also became acutely aware of a universal truth that children all over the world, laugh and cry in the same language—an international connection that was often overlooked.

The series had been popular with parents and children and was selected by teachers as supplemental reading for students in the early grades. But after the explosion of the nuclear family and subsequent scattering of members who regrouped in a variety of configurations with different titles and roles—full of terms like halfs—steps—singles— and extended, Harold's stories about the families of mice enjoying life's simple pleasures and courteous behavior were considered trite, stereotypical and passe'. Harold was stunned and mystified by the rapidly changing social patterns, values, rhythm and pace, and felt out of sync with the times. He also thought that for whatever reasons—for better or worse, the revolution had not been kind to its children.

Driving through the familiar countryside, on the same route traveled by his family when he was young, a pilgrimage on which his parents sought, through nature, a spiritual font to refill their dwindling, inner resources—a personal sanctuary, Harold began to think about his childhood and the combination of genes and environment that curiously made him feel an outcast. Harold had never thought of his parents as individuals with hopes and dreams of their own—with problems to resolve—needs to be met. They were just parents—shepherds of their family. He never appreciated the fact that they showed no disappointment in his lack of drive toward goals that would have made them outwardly proud. They had not attempted to hammer him into a niche for which he was ill suited, to achieve parental aggrandizement. They had merely spread out the passionate picnic of life saying, "Here it is—rich—nourishing—colorful— flavorful—some of it is probably not good for you—some too rich and potentially harmful—but pick and choose at your own discretion and one day you will strike a healthy balance.

Harold had not yet struck a balance. He was out of whack, and he knew it. But he did have an inner goal. He had been carrying around the nucleus of an idea but had not been able to see its full potential. He had allowed concern over the problem of his nonconformist attitudes to draw shades down on the work place of his mind. His goal was simple. He wanted to protect the children. Children whom he felt were bereft of a private and special childhood. He wanted to write a book so powerful that it would explode in the face of a generation who dumped its children and responsibilities on custodial caretakers— caregivers—surrogate parents—a cadre of non-familial personnel for which words had been cunningly concocted to simulate true feelings for what was best for the children. Harold thought the whole deal was a fraud—a cover-up—a paint job over the basic flaw of selfishness.

Harold had visited the Kiddie Kare Centers, shelters, and extended shelters with Honey on her rounds as a social worker. Each time, he was astonished to find the tender seedlings of a generation being bent, snapped and dropped here and there as if they were of no consequence in the grander scheme of "having it all."

Harold worried that these harried children being shuttled back and forth—here and there, would not have dream time—for special nurturing—would not be able to make storage space in the attics of their minds for their imaginations and recollections—that indeed the shackles of this lock step culture would inhibit their imaginations from developing and soaring to great heights because there was no one with the time or the inclination to provide the launching pad. Everyone was moving too fast—whizzing through a blur that distorted their vision.

The Relationship had heard it all before—in fact was living in the blur and feeling the pain of second string player, even as it sat in the car—eyes level with the widow ledge, watching clouds, tree tops and roofs sail by, like many other children—allowed to make the trip, but otherwise ignored, like excess baggage in the championship game of life. Good grief! The Relationship felt itself falling in league with Harold. It was shocked to see how quickly it was beginning to think like him—even (no way) playing the role of victim. This was risky business, the guy was a wuss on a trip to nowhere. The

Relationship needed to shore up its Harold acquired wobblies—toughen its wavering mind set and focus—focus—focus. That was the mantra of the day. The vision of Talk Show fame floated in the air and stuck to the surface of the window—reflecting an image of its powerful little self—seated in the guest chair of the highest rated Confessional in the Country.

Harold thought about the big empty houses that lined the streets across the country. It seemed strange to him that whole families did not live in them together, at the same time. The quiet shells, by day, were said to be occupied by part time inhabitants cruelly called, latchkey children, who wore a key to the house around their necks, but upon entering spent some trying times hiding under the beds, or in closets. For the adults, these trophy houses, built to fill a hole in themselves, were only used for weekends to unwind and evenings to get ready for the next stressful day, a pit stop on the way to nowhere. But these houses were scorecards—achievement grades—visible accounting of who and what the owners were and what they considered important. To the children they had passed along, with great pride, their self-induced disease called stress. A crippling— killing—mind twisting plague so incapacitating that it paralyzed the parts of the brain that had once known the difference between right and wrong—good and bad—needs and desires—love and lust. They were aware that this condition was caused by the mad, elbow banging scramble for position—for things—accoutrements—fleeting feel goods, which in the end, they knew, had little intrinsic value. But they couldn't stop. They were caught up—trapped—locked into a mindless sprint on tracks and lanes with dangerously accelerating speeds.

Harold wanted to tell them that the houses should not be scorecards, but homes full of laughter and love—where minds, bodies, and spirits were nourished and where time was measured out according to the seasons of life. That children deserved the season of childhood, unhurried—to grow into strong mature plants before the season of harvest. That the children should not be made mini adults, playing grown up games before they had the foundation that would protect them from the windstorms of life. Harold wondered if in their nerve jangling, all consuming quest, the upwardly mobile, ever thought of their own childhood—had some pleasant memories of peaceful days gone by—some remnants of their secret inner lives, that stirred their souls—gave strength and comfort in retrospect.

There was this attic in Harold's mind where he stored the treasures he had collected from childhood—startling untapped powers nestling in the shadows, a pure quality of courage—special mental gems and objects forged by pleasant memories and, imagination—uncut and unpolished—which he brought out to examine on rare occasions and shared only with Honey. Perhaps that was the problem with his writing—he kept the treasures locked up in the attic of his mind, when if he brought

45

them out and displayed them, others would say, "Hey, I thought about things like that, too. I had similar feelings. Odd isn't it? But precious stuff, too."

The Relationship rolled down the car window and leaned its head against the door. It needed fresh air. Harold's goal fumes were making it nauseous. He had a way of sucking the fun out of everything. It liked the idea of house scorecards—car scorecards—clothing scorecards—vacation scorecards. Keeping score was the only game in town. What fun was it if you only got one moon shot in a lifetime and you couldn't stick it to the also rans—show off your prizes—make them green with envy. Harold was a drone—a wet blanket on the real fuse of life—the spirit of competition, that fired off the canon signaling the race had begun. As they drove through the acres of former prairie and farmland observing the two-story look-a-like houses that sprouted on postage stamp lots, Harold put his arms around the steering wheel, his head low, and began to emit a strange wailing sound. Even at mid-day there were no children to be seen in the area once known as a neighborhood. The lawns, in previous times used for child's play, with arbors for hide and seek—trees for climbing, or building tree houses, were now landscaping statements—mini moats surrounding the fortresses once called homes, but currently referred to as properties, governed by committees. The children had been given all of the trappings purported to ensure the good life but little of the meaning. There wasn't time. And there was no need for family play yards. The land, buildings, equipment, and environment had been recreated at the Care Centers where the children spent their days, while the grown-ups drove back and forth, back and forth, in numbing isolation—mentally mouthing the mantra of the day, focus, focus on the deal. Faster, faster, never mind the wreckage along the roadway, someone would clean it up later.

Harold knew that he would have to stop the misdirected and perilous stream of traffic. Stand up like a highway patrolman at the scene of a disaster—man the barricades, swing the warning lanterns, and turn the drivers back—tell them to go home to their empty houses and find the children—free the children—protect the children—talk to the children—listen to the children. Help them form the treasures for the attic of their minds. But how was he to do this? Harold knew that he had never been good at arguing effectively with other adults—pressing a point—convincing someone that his views had merit. He would have to find a way. This would be his mission—his goal. If there was an answer to be found and a direction for his life, it could only be found at the sanctuary of the lake

At the family cottage, Harold laid a fire in the fireplace, threw his sleeping bag in front of it and pulled out the box of toys, saved from his childhood. There was the dump truck and his favorite travel loader with buckets attached to a chain link conveyor that scooped and dumped the sand into the

47

construction projects on the beach, when activated by a hand crank. There were games—carved driftwood—an assortment of shells and rocks and building blocks. The Relationship picked through the collection and turned up its nose, thankful that it had not been around in a time when manual labor toys were considered entertainment. It liked the power of video games— the zap-zapping of people and machines.

There was also the now defunct series of children's books written by Harold. They were lined up on a shelf in silent witness to a time gone by. Standing next to the series was a volume of Whittier's "Snowbound", that had been read and re-read by his parents when the family took winter weekends at the cottage. Respect and love of family and nature—those were the basic ingredients for building a solid foundation. The peace and beauty that came from the compatibility of the sustaining parts was very important to Harold. He believed in that combination—love and respect for others—for oneself—for family—for nature. These were the mortar and bricks that held one together when the windstorms of life hit—battered and beat down.

Harold lifted down a small box from the bookshelf that contained an outdated American flag and several flat, cardboard receptacles with round indentations that held the coins Harold collected when someone thought he might be interested in numismatics. He wasn't and the cards were only half filled. The

Relationship knew that Harold was about to embark on a search and destroy mission—probably about money. It felt a suffocating gloom permeate the air and decided to put some distance between itself and the purveyor of off-the-wall musings. It needed to protect its own interests from being sucked into this debilitating quagmire of moral concerns. It scurried to the safety of the front porch steps.

Harold picked up the small flag and twirled it around between his thumb and forefinger. He held up the flat of collected coins and began picking the round pieces of metal from their slots. There was that old, nagging phobia about money again—and the flag. But recently the problem had begun to form into a question. He knew that presidents loved the flag—honored the flag—made a big deal out of the flag and its aura. But there were no words printed on the flag—not like currency, that was engraved with the inspirational words, "In God We Trust".

Harold began to wonder if the words on the currency were much like the warning labels on alcohol and cigarettes—that the inspirational slogan was there to warn people to be cautious in the way they used their money. But then why would the government engrave, "In God We Trust" on the currency and then use the currency to subsidize the growing of grains, produce, and tobacco—from which were made the dangerous products that required warning labels—such as whiskey—gin—

and cigarettes? Harold thought that money was the most addictive and dangerous drug of all and needed a more straightforward and stronger warning than the vague, "In God We Trust." It seemed to him that if alcohol and tobacco were said to be dangerous to the health of one's mind and body and labeled as such, shouldn't the corruptive influence of money on the mind and spirit be similarly labeled as well? Why didn't the money read, "This May Be Dangerous to Your Moral Health?" And since money had been called the root of all evil and sometimes filthy lucre, wasn't there something grossly incongruous about mixing God— the evil root—and filthy lucre in the same pot? Harold also wondered, why after all the fracas about removing religion from the schools and the birth of Christ from the Christmas pageants, hadn't the government taken God off of the currency? If they were going to separate the Church from the State, why had they left God on the dirty coins and dollars that were made and distributed by the State? These kinds of obvious, but overlooked incongruities were disturbing to Harold. "In God We Trust," said Harold.

Who could he really trust, he wondered? He could trust Honey, he knew that. He could trust her with his life, and more importantly with his innermost thoughts. But could he trust himself? Harold put the toys away and went outside to inspect the long, horizontal tree limb that he and his brother had climbed and sat on while they dreamed their impossible dreams. It had served as a covered wagon—boat—horse—spaceship, and any vehicle their imaginations could conjure on their quest for the unreachable star. Memories of happy, uncomplicated times— freedom to wonder—flooded his mind. He climbed up and arranged himself with his back against the trunk and his legs stretched out along the smooth, white surface of the beech tree.

Harold's spirits soared when he was in this spot. He felt that he had the strength to go forth into the foray and whip the enemy at large—and in so doing, open up the bottleneck in his life. It also occurred to him that he was perhaps too much like his idol, Don Quixote, and might tilt at windmills forever, without success. This inability to bring his goal into focus and chart a course of action blurred his vision and made him feel weak and breathless. He slid down from the branch and went around the corner of the cottage to catch a refreshing lake breeze. The Relationship was still sitting on the porch steps, picking the round hats from acorns with its little fingers. Harold sat down next to the industrious creature. The Relationship took one look at Harold, all hunched and scowling with the burden of his ideas and slid away. It felt uneasy. Harold was getting quirky— anything could happen.

Suddenly Harold snatched the Relationship from the porch step and ran down the dune with the Relationship riding on Harold's shoulders, its arms wrapped tightly around his neck. Along the wet, firm edge of the shore, Harold raced wildly against the wind as if to blow the cloying problem away. He missed Honey—he wished she could be here to share the delicate days and twilight hours between summer and fall with all the promises of new beginnings stirring in the trees and bouncing off the waves. He missed her understanding heart—her sudden bursts of laughter. Harold truly loved Honey. He knew he could be gentle and kind to her—certainly loyal—even responsible. But it was too late. It wouldn't work—not with all the how-to books, and TV purveyors of pop- psyche, all speaking in Relationship Rap—pounding in his ears—causing a dizzying imbalance. And now this added uncertainty of not reaching his goal to save the children. He knew that Honey would be O.K. without him. She could find another Relationship. She was self reliant, desirable, lovable, loyal, trustworthy and sincere and utterly devoted to Harold, but there must be someone who had traveled the correct path and had achieved his goals, who would be more deserving of her incomparable love.

Tired and winded, Harold stopped and sat down on a log—the Relationship beside him. This had been a favorite place for Honey and Harold, when he was still in his advertising job and their love affair was fresh and new. The log served as the seating area for the audience and the beach was the stage for Honey's creative endeavors. She danced, sang and enacted commercials, selling everything from her beautiful sand castles—"This lovely forty-five room lake front castle has been upgraded to include—" and as the waves washed over the sand castle—"running water in every room—" to sunsets—"Get 'em while they're hot. These mega-watt toasties have the capacity to dry, fry and bake a pie. No two sets are alike. Batteries are made in heaven." As the fiery, red sun extinguished itself in the lake and one could almost hear the sizzle of heat hitting water, Honey would touch a finger to her tongue and provide the appropriate sound—Pissst. Then she would dip down, like a ballerina, pick up an edge of her long, gauzy beach dress, twirl around and leap through the air—blond hair swinging in the breeze—this way and the other—a sea nymph reflecting the beauty of her surroundings.

In all of Honeys' actions, joy spun out from her heart with centrifugal energy to her sensitive and talented hands—enabling her to express herself as fluently as a mime or a hula dancer telling beautiful stories with gestures articulating grace and reverence. Love was the commodity she traded openly. It was at these times that Harold could hardly bear the pain of loving her. Those insistent memories swirled about him in a kind of ethereal vortex that drew the image of his beloved close enough to reach out and embrace. Then, spinning together in a powerful, momentary eddy, the dream ended without a conclusion.

He visualized Honey being tossed about with him and he feared for her safe passage. He wanted to drop a protective shield over her, so that no one could ever hurt her. He also wondered why, then, he had been selected to do that very thing. What horrid, perfidious twist of some major control had plopped him in this hopeless position—to inflict the unthinkable wound on the beautiful, innocent, Honey. He knew then that he would have to remain separated from her so that he would not bring her down with him when he failed to reach his goal.

As they sat there on the log, the Relationship's funk began to expand into a full blown depression. It wasn't cognizant of these happier times that Harold conjured up. Some part of it must have been there—under a different name—like Love, perhaps, but its metamorphosis had not surfaced until later, when the skittish folks dumped all their fears of flying and falling on its tiny back. The Relationship—born of default—no hits, no runs, no errors. What a legacy. What a birthright.

It was at times like this the Relationship felt like an unwanted child whose presence spoiled the pleasure and romance once shared by the couple. This incipient reminder of its humble beginnings tended to grind it down. It had to keep its own Star Search goals in mind. Flame the desire to reach the top. Dredge up crud from the past to plaster its way to success. Throw in dysfunctional and low self esteem, then simper down and suck up. Attain stardom for being a plucky little survivor. Those Talk Show people ate that stuff up. Oh, God, it could hardly wait. Still, at the moment, the Relationship would probably have to sit quietly until Harold's meandrous thoughts about Honey wound themselves out.

When Harold began to spin out the reels in his mind's eye, he saw Honey appear as if in a home movie—flickering on the invisible screen. "God, those beautiful, healing hands," Harold said aloud. Honey's hands had a mesmerizing effect on Harold. He felt an electrical current surging through his body. To watch those magical hands at work— folding the laundry, smoothing the towels and linens—pressing, patting, caressing, blessing— even at a distance could cause a major meltdown of his spinal column and connected nerve endings. At times like that, seeing Harold watching her, Honey would hold a fluffy towel against her cheek and announce, "Pick up a box of Soap-So-Dear and experience the serenity of tradition. Soap-So-Dear, a trusted family friend for over one hundred years." Then lapsing into her little girl voice, "Umm, this smells like grandma's house. I wuv Soap-So-Dear."

"God, those beautiful, healing hands," cried Harold again.

Startled, the Relationship gave up skipping stones on the water and sat back on the log, while visions of sugar plums danced in its head—and exploded in a burst of reality fallout.

The Relationship wondered sometimes if Honey's selflessness showed some kind of character fault—a crack that she was trying to fill with over compensation—too much goodness was suspect in today's market. It suggested a sign that she may have suffered some kind of childhood trauma—possibly a doll she wanted for Christmas, that missed the sleigh ride to her house and left a baleful, unrequited longing, deep in her beautiful round skull.   That was the kind of thing that altered adult behavior—denial—it was very popular in the annals of poop psychology.   Almost everybody had a major complaint from childhood—a bummed out feeling large enough to hang some weirdness on—and make it stick.

The Relationship thought that if the sainted Sister Theresa's background was carefully examined, there might possibly appear some kind of gross disappointment. Perhaps, zero dates for the prom, or a cruel cut from the cheerleading squad. Her outfit and the "do" suggested as much. Something could have been done with the eyes though. They were good—expressive—kind—intelligent. Some mascara or liner might have worked.   Still, living a saintly life must have some merits—if you liked the grunt work. But in today's climate nobody was all that kind and giving or even capable of success without a whack of some sort from childhood. Speaking from the swollen, porked out point of view of self gratification—trying too hard to please was not the kind of attribute that garnered success as it was currently defined.   And yet, in spite of Honey's full plate of accomplishments and the pleasure with which she exercised her many skills, the Relationship, noticed that she frequently paused in mid flight, her eyes spacing around, searching for the missing piece of her puzzle—that elusive cut-out from the center of the picture of her life.

Harold, still seated on the log, watching the Honey movie reel out, elbows on his knees—chin resting on knuckled hands—suddenly laughed. He was recounting the complex circuitry of Honey's mind. She had a problem with words. There was something a hair off in her selection process of verbal expressions resulting in her use of words that sounded close to the meaning she intended, but actually describing a corollary and slightly comical, interpretation. Still, there was always an intricate and interesting connection between the words that drew an imperfect picture with a stubborn resonance. In fact placed an indelible stamp on certain cliches—lending a refreshing twist to otherwise boring commentary that was not easily forgotten.

At first friends and co-workers were put off by this strange malfunction and wondered if Honey really grasped the subject she was attempting to discuss. But over time they became impressed with her ability to organize the most complex concepts— bring chaos into order and generally come up with carefully thought out programs to enhance the welfare of all she encountered. The word "dyspepsia" as she called it, had an endearing quality and provided a point of reference that stuck in people's minds— colorful word pictures, absent of stereotypes, which left an imprint of a complete story. Honeyisms were quoted throughout the landscape where she traveled. And a lot of happy faces trailed after her.

Harold smiled remembering the "dyspepsia" remark. It was one of his favorites that showed the interconnecting components of Honey's mind. She once told Harold about a couple of her acquaintance whose only furniture consisted of a few floor pillows and a double tofu. Harold understood immediately that the correct word was futon, because in Honey's purview, people who lived sparsely and slept on a futon probably were health conscious and therefore ate tofu. And had she mentioned that they were very congealed, (as in together and friendly). Pulling her car into a space immediately in front of the local super market, one day, Honey exclaimed, "Look, Harold, gourmet parking." It figures. Such was Honey's off center world of unforgettable, verbal picture painting.

Harold got up from the log, lifted the Relationship back on his shoulders and began to walk swiftly through the water's rivulets along the edge of the beach His concentration was still on Honey and his connection with her, it was as if all the sights he treasured were refractions of her beauty.. The Relationship saw the light bulb of an idea flash on over Harold's head and knew that he was back on the treasures of the attic of his mind. Harold knew that Honey had treasures in the attic of her mind, too, collected from childhood. Items from her grandmother— fragrance of jams, jellies, pickles and sauces—breads and pies—

warm kitchen conversations The aroma of well being was the catalyst that jogged the memories into active duty for a needed lift during personal down time. And the key was to value the process of work as well as the outcome—that the spirit in which tasks were performed made a happy life. In all of Honey's actions, she carried the presence of home about her—a place that was good to be in—a place that lonely people sought to make sure they still belonged in the safety zone of human kindness—where eddies of winged creatures lead to paths of floating clouds— counterpanes on which quiet times allowed individuals a chance to rest—to be themselves and adjust to the rhythms of life and love.

As Harold's pace quickened, the Relationship felt a new kind of energy surge through him. Harold was on to something.. His inner and outer goals were connecting. He turned abruptly and raced up the dune shouting, "I will write the book. I will write the book." Then reaching the pinnacle, he turned toward the lake and spoke triumphantly into the wind. "I will reach them through the treasures in the attic of their minds, where the strengths of childhood are stored. Once again, shouting this time over the breaking waves and the clapping tree tops. "I will show them how to select and gather the treasures—how to place them in order of their protective qualities—for future times when the windstorms of life arise and attack. These will be the amulets, the talismans, the badges—assembled in a mighty structure of incomparable strength and beauty—not to ward off the windstorms, but to weather them."

Then stepping back, Harold said, "Courage, I shall place that treasure on top for it will be the one most needed and most effective. It would be composed of special words and phrases—poems and psalms—sounds and scents from the crackling fires of fall to the healing power of puppy breath. Courage, the pristine amulet of valor." Harold was trembling as if he was about to embark on an out of body experience—that he might suddenly lift off and soar up into the stratosphere with the Relationship clinging to his neck, flapping in the breeze like Superman's cape. " 'Courage," Harold intoned, "'is the price that Life exacts for granting peace, the soul that knows it not. Knows no release from little things' "—"Each time we make a choice, we pay with courage to behold resistless day, and count it fair.' " That was the message his mother quoted frequently from a poem, by her idol, Amelia Earhart. And it was the message to be voiced through the pages of The Treasures In the Attic of Your Mind.

The Relationship shuddered. In all of Harold's pontificating it failed to see the humor in the delivery. Was the mention of puppy breath supposed to fill that necessary requirement, to help carry the heavy load? Harold pulled the Relationship from his shoulders and dropped it on the ground.

He retrieved his gear from the cottage, tossed it in the car and took off.

The Relationship, momentarily dazed from the dumping, scrambled to its feet and ran after the car. It slipped, fell to its knees and began to cry. It wanted to go back to Honey. It was frightened and alone. A gust of cold air whipped against its tired little body. It knew it was down for the count. It felt itself expiring and wondered if it passed on, would it rise again like a Phoenix from the flames? The Relationship shuddered. It was afraid of fire and it didn't believe in reincarnation. It needed a connection to survive. Were there any options? Had it a few untapped resources left to pull out of this horror?

Suddenly it remembered seeing a beautiful young woman sitting alone on the beach—a sketch pad and pencils in a case beside her. She was dressed in a white sleeveless blouse and jeans rolled up to reveal slender, sun tanned, arms and legs. Her dark hair was gathered into a long shiny taper tied with a leather thong and hanging down in front of her left shoulder.

With every ounce of its dwindling strength, the Relationship pulled itself up and began crawling to the edge of the dune. Then it slid down on its stomach and oozed over to the lovely lady. It sat down so close, it was touching her arm. It gazed up into her face with the most endearing and vulnerable smile it could muster. The woman seemed receptive. She put her arm around the Relationship—returned the smile and drew it closer.

The Relationship snuggled up and breathed a sigh of relief. This was always the way the game started out. Warm and cuddly—open—innocent—trusting—caring— comfortable— content. This was O.K .for the moment, but in the back of its head plans were forming—deals were being cast. There were still mountains to climb—places to go—important people to work on. Stardom was once again in its future. The vision of its Talk Show appearance flickered on the screen in a dream sequence—pressing the button on the power pump to its brain. The scheming had begun. Sitting side by side in the dusky aura of eventide, the beautiful, dark haired, self-contained lady was unaware of the inescapable link between them.

The Mysterious
Painting

The Artist Lady Draws Attention

The Relationship was winded as it followed the long strides of the pretty artist lady up the steep, arduous climb to the top of the dune. Its heart was pounding, and its tired, little legs trembling and it was unnerved by the fact that she had not even once looked back to see if it was O.K. This was a new experience for the Relationship— Honey had always checked on its condition. What kind of person was this?

The two story, stone, glass and wood house grew up out of the sand and dune grass amid towering, heavy leafed, oak and beech trees and fragrant pines. The structure had not been visible from the beach because it reflected the foliage and sky and appeared to be an extension of the natural surroundings—it

63

was a sculpture sprung complete from the earth. In its altered state, the house was an artistic compliment to its origins—as if the glass and wood, having been transformed from melted sand and hewn logs were paying homage to the living vegetation—in a state of grace.

When they entered the house, the light from the answering machine was blinking from the surface of a round Florentine table in the stark living room/studio. The artist ignored the electronic summons and quickly ascended the spiral staircase to the bedroom loft, where she changed into a colorful caftan and released her hair from the leather thong. The Relationship sank into the canvas butterfly chair in the sparsely furnished quarters. It was totally exhausted and a little frightened by this independent artist woman.

As it sat in a torpor, induced by hunger and fear, observing the interior of the glass house, it was surprised that there were no paintings of surf and sand—sunsets over the water—autumnal foliage, or melancholy dune grass.

The interior walls were bare—nothing hanging from, or leaning against them. The only example of the artist's work was a single, large canvas, propped up on an easel, that dominated the entire room. It was not, as would have been expected—a reproduction of the abundantly available scenes of nature. Instead, the painting was a startlingly provocative mood piece— that seemed to emanate power waves from its surface.

The Relationship squinted its eyes and peeked through its little fingers at the mysterious canvas—and shivered. The painting was a compelling depiction of the critical role inanimate objects play in defining our contemporary culture. The diversity of the leading characters, was the current enigma. The Relationship felt a worrisome resonance fluttering through the air—an unspecified prelude to disaster, bouncing off the electrified face of the painting.

The story of the leading characters, unfolds against a background of rugged, burnt orange, sandstone walls and dark charcoal shadows, resembling a canyon reflecting a sunset — with a splash of bright yellow streaming through the mysterious atmosphere. The scene was not a naturescape, but a replica of the artist's studio.

The canvas, with its mysterious style of overlapping strokes of light and dark— focusing the eye along a path, building to a bold and again mysterious crescendo— revealed, at first, a white laminated drafting table, with an attached, black metal, flex-lamp on one side—its beam focussed on drawing materials and instruments of calibration, carefully arranged on the flat surface.

The scooped out, leading edge of the table, designed to hold pens and pencils, currently doubled as a clothing rack, supporting a row of hangers draped with freshly laundered blouses and shirts. Then, looming out of the surrounding shadows was a slender, fragile, ironing board on which stood the face of a shining iron—its dangling, dark cord disconnected from its source of energy in the wall, seemed to be casting about for some visually obscure new connection with the drafting table. Possibly a covert mission to tap into a perceivably higher voltage—or perhaps a power joust between the domestic field and the commercial. Or were the searching, sharp pronged, eyes, protruding from the plug, simply seeking equality, compatibility, understanding, appreciation, for the pleasure in ironing a perfect shirt as opposed to executing the perfect architectural rendering. Still the ironing board's seemingly uncertain role suggested an uneasy alliance with the sturdy, sleek, dominating, drafting table.

The Relationship thought the drafting table, standing firm and square against the rough hewn, vertical beams and sandstone wall, was a guy thing—thought the collection of girl stuff was intruding on the male turf—slyly marking her territory. It wondered if the artist was stating a role preference—at least in line of importance to herself. To a gender conscious eye, the drafting table playing the traditional male role and the enigmatic ironing board, the female, suggested that she favored them both with equal care and consideration, but that the quandary was yet to be resolved..

Sucked into the aura of the painting, the Relationship was startled by the return of the artist. The woman glided silently across the floor, in bare feet, then standing in front of the canvas, began to busy herself with palette, paint and brushes—carefully applying supporting strokes to shore up the under carriage of the wavering ironing board. Abruptly she turned, as if noticing the blinking light on the telephone equipment for the first time. She pressed the button releasing the voice message. The Relationship was impressed. Honey always checked her answering machine the minute they entered her house, or she would pick up the receiver after only one ring, just in case it might be an important call from Harold. Laura's telephone equipment did not require a hand held instrument to transmit the messages. Instead, a voice spoke out to the entire room.

"Hi, Laura, Charlie here. Everything is set up for the Opening. I can't wait to see the finished product. Everyone here is dying of curiosity. The title alone has all the critics and art lovers breathless. I know it is going to make a dynamite statement for women. It's already causing quite a stir."

Before sending her own message, Laura gave the Relationship a curious glance, then disappeared into the high tech galley and returned with a bowl of fruit and a plate of nutri-biscuits which consisted of flat little squares of grains and seeds that had been hammered into pulp and glued together with mortar from hell. Laura placed the plate of food on the black lacquered, dining table, picked up a nutri-brick and began to nibble the edges, then motioned to the pathetic little waif to dive in. The Relationship was too weak to peel an orange or press its little teeth through the skin of an apple, so it crawled onto the table, selected a small bunch of grapes, one of the pressed, plywood biscuits, and returned to the chair.

Laura moved around in front of the painting, viewing it from different angles, then glancing at the metal, plaque that held the provocative title of the commanding picture, she said, "Dichotomy/Compatibility/Versatility." Turning to the phone machine, she tapped out Charlie's number. Three rings sounded in the quiet room, then Charlie's voice, "Art is the substance of life that separates the excellent from the ordinary."

"No kidding. I thought Art was the substance that separated collectors from their money. "Laura said.

"Hey, let's not cast aspersions on our daily bread," Charlie said. "Or is it, don't cast bread on our daily aspersions? Gee, are we having fun already?"

"Not in this wing of the palace, Dear Heart. I'm having a problem with the title. I don't like it anymore. I mean, Dichotomy/Compatibility/Versatility? It seems self-serving. It's too heavy handed. I don't want to bash people over the head to get a reaction. I want them to see and feel something of their own life in this. Also, I'm not trying to define a woman's role or sympathize with it. I don't see them as victims. We all have tasks to perform, but the mind is free to choose where it works and plays. Everyone has a responsibility to help level the playing field—if it takes a major pounce on one side of the field to make the other end pop up—or if it just takes a tweak or torque to flatten it into some semblance of an equal scrambling surface, do it.

"Anyway, it's not just the finished product of the task that is paramount, but the ongoing mental processes free to conjure up improbable and impossible dreams that is significant. It doesn't matter whether the playing field is a drafting table or an ironing board, the spiritual playing field is always level."

"Whoa, you're going too fast and too deep for me," said Charlie. "Can we back up a bit and get this thing into some kind of perspective, especially one that simple minded ol' me can understand?"

"Don't be sappy, Charlie, you know darn well what I'm talking about, but your bottom line is different than mine. You were even rude enough to refer to my work as a product. Where have you been hanging out?" said Laura.

"O.K, so we're not having fun, yet. But let's get to the real kernel. It's not about what I said, is it?" said Charlie.

"Actually, no. It's just that, lately, the painting seems like my autobiography staring me in the face—the story of my life, my feelings, and my innermost thoughts — plastered on a canvas for all the world to see. I think I'm becoming over-protective, even a little reluctant about letting it go. Any gross misunderstanding of the portrayal would be tough to take.

"Anyway, I've been thinking a lot about my grandmother. She performed such a variety of tasks, most of them in an alcove she designed to hold the "boxes of her endeavors," as she called them. Each chore, or hobby had a coordinating container in her head that opened and closed just as each imaginary box at her finger tips was opened until the task had been completed and then closed to work on the next project Nothing was allowed to spill out of one box into another. None of the boxes was labeled in order of some quasi level of importance. She kept the books for my grandfather's candy factory, precisely, and accurately. She embroidered intricate designs on tea towels and pillow cases. She wrote copious notes and letters to friends and relatives, organizations and politicians—maintained a journal of personal thoughts, family life, national and community goings on—in a wry humor that was hilarious to every one fortunate enough to read from it.

"She checked the workers in the candy factory to see if they were fairly treated and compensated. She carried on a running dialogue with the women candy makers. "So, Elsie," she would say. "How are the nougats today?" "Thick and stubborn, as usual," was the answer. "They hate being covered with chocolate. It makes them feel unappreciated." She jotted down recipes that would be tested in her other domain—the kitchen. At the end of the day she would collect all of the worries, disappointments, and hurtful thoughts—give them careful consideration, solve the solvable—and put the rest in the last box, and mentally step on it. She had no patience with anyone indulging in self pity. Whining was a sound she couldn't abide. She would say, 'Don't whine, bark if you have a complaint.'"

"I remember your Grandmother," Charlie said, "She was definitely a top contender in the fly weight division."

"You've got that right. She always spoke with such authority." said Laura. "But my favorite memory of her is the time when I was ten and competed in the Silver Skate races in our town. It had been warm for several days before the race causing the top layer of ice to melt. But the judges decided not to postpone the races, which left us to skate through two inches of water on top of the ice. About halfway through the course I fell down and was sliding along on my backside, clocking a pretty good time, when a voice piercing through the heavy damp air, instructed me to 'Get up, you can still win.'

"And so I did, get up and I did, win. As it turned out the other skaters who had been ahead of me, also fell down. But they did not get up, since they were without benefit of my Grandmother's incredible direction. "I miss her, I need her down here. I could use her direction and a good laugh."

"She is down here, Laura, her presence is in your painting, I can feel it," said Charlie.

"Thanks for that," Laura said, "but I can't see her special humor in the picture."

"Without taking away from the importance of the message, I've always thought that the ironing board was probably laughing, or at least about to kick its heels together while the drafting table looked on with delight. In fact I've wondered about the dialogue between the two characters."

"I can only imagine, but I hope their attitude shows the Compatibility part of the title," said Laura.

The Relationship, suffering from loneliness and starvation plus the strain of witnessing their, foreign exchange, felt a lump in its throat and tears close to spilling out. It was homesick. After its arduous day, it would like to have had some comfort food—possibly a dish of mashed potatoes with rich golden gravy or a generous helping of Honey's home time spaghetti, or a bowl of warm porridge with currants and sweet cream that eased everyone into a relaxed state of somnolence. Honey called it her Dream Soup.

The Relationship missed Honey, possibly even Harold, but it knew it had to persevere. It was time to repeat the motivating words—Fame and Fortune, Fame and Fortune. Like the man said it takes guts and drive. The Get Up You Can Still Win, mantra, passed down from the grandmother wasn't a bad motivator either. It would use it in the future when rounding the curves of its own life cycle. A rush of excitement and power surged through its veins. It would find the artist's buttons and begin to press. She had to have "those buttons", everybody did. Still, this Charlie character was beginning to look like a better prospect for the next mark. He was no doubt where the money was.

Charlie's voice returned in a subdued tone, "Look, I'm sorry, Laura, I know how important this painting is to you, but I feel sure that even as I saw it last week, the mood, the color, and the subject conveys the dilemma of this generation of women that you are addressing. It really projects a bridge to understanding, provocative because the enigma is not totally spelled out. It's as you say, up to the individual to solve the equation as it applies to her own life. That's what will make the painting immortal. There will always be that question. You know. Is the Mona Lisa smiling, or no?"

"Possibly, but at the moment I'm having second thoughts about the role of the ironing board. It looks weak and needy, and insecure. I want it to show a kind of traditional grace. A reflection of the times when it touched the most intricate embroidered linens, hand stitched with pride and joy. I want it to feel confident. There really should be a resolution of sorts. Maybe that would be a better title, or do you think Harmony is better? If there is too much conflict in the painting and the title, perhaps the best thing to do is just call it "Resolution." I'd like to believe the conflict is resolved in the picture," Laura said.

"I'm afraid it's too late to change it now, all of the print material has been out for weeks. Not to worry, the painting stands on its own. Gotta go, make sure the piece de resistance is

73

carefully crated and sent by special messenger to the gallery—well you know the deal. I'll have my limo pick you up at the lake house and I'll meet you later at the gallery. Trust me, this is going to be one hell of a successful exhibit. Take care," said Charlie and signed off.

On the drive to the city, the Relationship wallowed in the comfortable, cushy, back seat of the long, white, stretch limo, as it sped along the highway. It looked around at the interior appointments—the bar—the small refrigerator—the desk with the stationary rolodex that flipped down into a storage deck—the cellular phone—the tiny TV with its cable connection flashing spasms of stock quotations, and it knew it had arrived—knew in its heart of hearts that this was where it belonged. This was what it had waited for—a big time deal—access to the world of dynamics—money—power—control.

Laura, quiet and in some kind of subjective mood, gazed out the window on her side of the car. She paused momentarily to glance at the Relationship, then opened the refrigerator, which had been thoughtfully stocked by Charlie with her personal beverage preferences, and selected a small bottle of mixed vegetable juices. She offered the drink to the Relationship and gently patted its little leg—drawing a simpy grin from the pathetic parasite.

Feeling a shot of confidence, delivered via the veggie cocktail and the affectionate pat, the Relationship quietly—so as not to disturb the once again pensive and distant Laura, began to spin through the numbers—names—and codes listed on the Rolodex cards. It took a pen and note paper from the desk to jot down the information, then stuffed the notes in its survival kit. This was the kind of pay dirt it had been hoping to find—a way to manipulate the numbers into a cache of its own. With time and stealth, it could pull off a national bonanza. The Relationship sniggered at the wide open possibilities for up-grade and snuggled down into the euphoria of greed dreams.

Exhibiting Art—of All Kinds

At the gala opening of Laura's well publicized exhibit, the "Dichotomy" painting, as it was currently called—had been launched into a sea of art lovers—buyers— dealers—critics, and society mavens. It floated on an easel in the center of the art gallery—dramatically lighted and situated—where throngs of curious patrons gazed— puzzled—wondered and commented on the complex canvas. Then turning away, in search of a less commanding exhibition of the artist's work, the spectators found wonder and enchantment in Laura's naturescapes, with special recognition of the winter scene entitled, "Wintersurf," a near photo image of a wave frozen in mid break— suspended and covered with snow, but with the outline of the scroll still visible. It evoked a sense of eternity—life frozen in a time frame—hope and serenity—a chance for transformation. But then they returned for a second look—an in-depth examination of the compelling "Dichotomy," to find a personal revelation—each observer drawing a different interconnecting experience and interpretation.

Meanwhile, the Relationship moved and grooved among the rich and famous—working the crowd—glad handing— sucking up—pressing people that could make a difference— tuning into private conversations, and secreting notes in its survival kit. Its little legs pumping in, through, and around the throngs, so it could grab whatever it thought it deserved and had been denied.

Laura, entered regally in a simple, floor length knit gown, interwoven with shimmering, silver threads. Her dark hair twisted and studded with glittering faux jewels—became its own magnificent tiara. In fond attendance at her side was the impeccable Charlie—handsome—charming—witty—worldly—protector—promoter— co-star. He zigged and zagged—directing the energy and enthusiasm of the gathering toward the shy and socially reluctant Laura, whose tolerance for public display was, at best, minimal. Still to the world they were the "cake top" couple, the art circle's match of the moment—the magnet that drew the extras in the drama into focus for the chance to be seen where "They" were—even as background in a society photo—drinks in hand— smiling into the camera. Such was the suction of celebrity grouping. And the Relationship shared in their bright, shining hour.

But it was the "hour" business that bothered the Relationship. It had an uneasy feeling that this glamorous duo's arrangement was fleeting—or part time. The connection appeared to be uneven—lop-sided—one-sided—or perhaps it was a business- friendship deal—without the love thing. In fact, as the Relationship toured Laura's paintings, amid its power run, it could see that something was missing. In spite of the exquisite portrayal of love, strength, and beauty of nature in her paintings—the balance of energy and peace—and her profound belief in fairness—the importance of respectful coexistence among species—there was a hole somewhere. There was that unsettling poignancy in the way the wave broke in the "Wintersurf" painting—pulling at raw emotions— suggesting a heart breaking at the crest. Or the shadowy, iron cord in "Dichotomy," searching for an elusive connection.

The Relationship thought that the missing element was the big "L", love, a la Honey and Harold—the imponderable something that sparked a flame between a man and a woman. Perhaps that missing part was the compelling factor in Laura's art. The element that was not there, posed as the starring member because of its absence—and spurred the unending search—the powerful quest to find the pattern of one's own life.

The Relationship knew that this kind of association was dragging it down. It couldn't afford to get emotionally involved with Laura's quest or cause. It had to split from the debilitating drama of this dead-end street—get on with its own agenda— hook up with a top team that would carry it to dizzying heights— people recognized through the, so called, civilized world, as super shakers. There must be someone at that level, right here, in this gathering. It had heard some big names tossed about— listened in on some fairly large transactions being negotiated. Hell, it had to give it another shot— waltz around one more time—ride herd on the masses and separate out the winning couple, who would pave the way for its mission.

And there they were—the mega industrial titan—real estate magnate, Larry Lamp, Lawrence, or Lawless, as some called him, whose light shone on his vast international holdings on every day—and his latest adornment, a full size Barbie in a doll size dress, standing in front of the "Dichotomy," looking intently at the canvas, as if they could grasp the meaning—and if they did, would they care about the subject? The Relationship knew they hadn't arrived at the pinnacle of success, as it was currently defined, by wasting time contemplating the inequality of life. That was for slow people—dreamers, like Harold, Honey, and Laura, who slogged along trying to fix things that weren't broke.

Not this couple, the Lamp had caught the tail of a rising meteor and ridden it all the way, and she was simply the vapor carried along to catch the dazzling, luminous, fallout in her ready little pocket At last the perfect vehicle for its own moon shot. The Relationship quickly insinuated itself between the flagrant hotel magnate—casino operator—airline owner—face man—hot shot, and his clinging arm candy, while they were blinded by popping flash bulbs and distracted by reporters. The dynamic duo unknowingly, but instantly became the triple threat, as the Relationship stuck its face between them at every click of the cameras. A threesome strutting their stuff, captured flaunting their fame on film for posterity—the Relationship of the World's

Most Famous Couple became the World's Most Famous Relationship, poised like a rocket to explode on the daytime Talk Show circuit, with its bag of secret crud. Oh wonder of wonders, its train was finally leaving the station. Next stop—fame, fortune and payback.

Still happily dazed by the commingling with the dream team, the Relationship was not immediately cognizant of the drama unfolding on center stage.

The recently minted Barbie Doll, still draped over the titan's arm, and standing in front of the Dichotomy painting, seemed to be performing a warm up gig to rally the crowd for the main event. As art patrons gathered like moths around a light, Babs began her ritual of the mouth, a mesmerizing routine that called attention to her special talents. It was a precision act carried out in perfect sequence. While still holding the stem of the wine flute and cocktail napkin supporting a crab puff, in one hand, she pinched the teensiest smidgen from the canapé and pushed it in her barely opened, aperture, with the other. Those busy little fingers, stuck in every pie and mouth—then fed a morsel to the mogul and repeated the ritual. Pinch, push—pinch, push—oops a crumb lingers seductively on the curl of his lower lip. Flick, flick, out comes the pointed tip of her baby tongue— misses, requiring a helpful nudge from little third finger. The audience totally enraptured with the picking and licking was now focused for the big show—a bombshell of shattering cultural icons.

The gallery patrons were startled into a group paroxysm—their combined gasp of air threatening to implode the entire facility, when the airhead apparent, came precariously close to the canvas with her wine flute. Then releasing her not seriously grown-up, little pinky finger from the glass, began to waggle it at various parts of the painting. Her power of concentration, cribbed on her frontal lobe for easy pickings and trained to deliver the final act, for its utmost value, was attempting to bring forth an original interpretation. The translation, culled from her limited exposure to pictures, without people in graphic poses, took some doing.. It would be a tough call. She would have to transpose the subjects—hardware for soft physical counterparts— in order to make a statement.

Still snaking the intrepid little digit, along the surface of the canvas, in her personal conception—she surveyed the formidable, dark alcove—the moody shadows— the sleek, intimidating drafting table, decked with image stalking, instruments on top and discarded clothing draped along side—focussed briefly on the obviously sex starved, face of the glaring, iron with its implicit orgiastic intent on outrageous punishment—examined the anxious wall socket, voyeuristically peeking from slit eyes—traced the dangling, groping cord to the pulsating, erotic power plug. Then with held-breath tension, thrust the titillating, instructional, little pointer between the three prongs, and delivered her cutesy, slam dunk rendition. "Its kinky," she squealed, and spun back into the open arms of the magnate who squeezed his dolly even tighter than her spandex mini dress, as she placed the tip of her little appendage in his mouth, attempting to incite an electrical current that once would have started a conflagration through those parts of his body, but now seemed blocked by a stronger element.

In that instant Larry Lamp knew, even as he whipped out his checkbook, that the acquisition of the Dichotomy painting portended a new and strange departure and a quest for a rare encounter he had never imagined.

Charlie was immobilized by the sheer crassness of the event. The Relationship felt a wave of nausea burbling up in its esophagus, but Laura, having caught sight of the fandango, knew exactly the proper procedure to follow. She strode across the foyer in her regal, tiara topped elegance—then executing the most unprecedented move in art circles, lifted the painting from the easel and said, "No way, Jose'," and proceeded to cart the canvas off through the startled throngs of people to the main exit of the gallery.

As she waltzed off with the "Dichotomy" tucked firmly under her right arm, her left hand flew up and pulled the braided tiara apart, loosening the faux jewels, scattering the colorful baubles in her wake. The beautiful dark hair bounced free and swung defiantly, heralding the great escape from the phony baloney. The canvas- napping and free-fall hair statement made by the fleeing Laura, would leave an indelible print on the collective retina of the art community's eye. The community's eye turned abruptly to focus on the scene of the crime, where Charlie stood in front of the empty easel, smiling broadly and shaking his head. He was unflappable in the face of a possible disaster and not totally surprised by Laura's actions. "What a woman," he said, and followed his pounding heart toward the exit, where with unbelievable coincidence, the Relationship spotted Harold bounding for the same departure zone—the beautiful "Winterscape" firmly held in both hands, as he attempted to push open the door with his backside. The mope was actually smiling and babbling.

The Relationship always thought Harold was a mental cliff hanger, or was the guy singing? Nah, Harold couldn't carry a tune in a bushel basket. Still, while the words were on his lips, the music was surely in his heart.

There was no doubt the exquisite painting was meant for Honey. But would she be ready for the new Harold—the melancholy misfit, who had finally found a reason to smile and sing? Honey had her own box of rocks to sort out. The Relationship felt a pang of loneliness, and wondered where Honey was and if she ever thought of it in a kindly way. Maybe missed it just a little.

The Mogul and Babe, unaccustomed to surprises at their expense and the ensuing commotion, caused by the fleeing Laura. And with the painting not in their possession, looked profoundly moved by their brief encounter with the Dichotomy. In fact the titan of industry seemed momentarily struck, as if a thought process he had kept at bay, was attempting to break free, and pull him along with it—to parts unknown.

And the Barbie's courage to let her spirit roam free through her mental junk yard and extract a pearl of such enormous attraction, from the cumulative detritus of her experience, bought her a "place in time" of epic proportions on the underside of graphic presentations.

As for the Lamp, he had already had it all—the money, the fame, the power, the notoriety, the wives and children. Everybody wanted something from him—a piece of the action, or of himself, and the challenges were no longer alluring. What more was there to conquer? The thought startled him and began to gnaw away at the inner sanctum of his brain. Simplify, simplify, simplify, that would be his new credo. Go back to that part of being young without all of the taboos and the race to get where the action was—to prove something to someone— everyone—to control enough of the universe, so that his name would never be forgotten—Larry Lamp, shining from towers all over the world.

But now, he wanted to head back down the road—in an open car—along the country by-ways—in late fall , absorbing the burnished landscape through newly heightened senses—to pull from this gentle land a purity of spirit he had never known. He would find the lonely roads left behind by prosperity to fend for themselves. Roads, that people once enjoyed and finally revered for the endless opportunity to create a land of worthy refinement. Then, unceremoniously scrapped for the wider, faster modes of travel where getting to and from was the important thing. All the sights and sounds in between were of little consequence to the speeding masses.

These old roads were said to have calming powers—healing powers, and stretches that rolled out like a welcoming carpet to facilitate this new leafy, lofty learning curve. Roads tended by people who filled the potholes and cracks in their lives and counted it fair. These were not the movers and shakers and expansionists. They were the maintenance people who kept the earth glued together for the next generation.

Why, at this particular time and place, was the mogul suddenly overcome with a weakening of resolve—a fleeting sense of relief, that there was something outside of himself directing him to an alien but compelling destiny. Was it the way the artist, with such grace and elan, hauled out her painting to protect its integrity, that struck a discord in his previously harmonious existence?

He had been sensing a change in the wind—breezes blowing away lines drawn in the sand, and attitudes he thought were carved in stone, cracking apart. His legs felt the ground beneath him shake, but he would doubtless weather the storm— at least until the conclusion of the most important mega-deal he had ever put together. He would always honor his commitments even though the tingling up his spine was arresting. He had, after all, sprung full bloom from family roots that had been cultivated specifically to grow wealth and comfort. And in his turn he had pruned, spliced, and grafted young shoots to mature growth, resulting in the overall strength of the enterprises. In so doing, he had become the international mergers and acquisitions titan, acclaimed for his own personal style, now known as shake, quake, and take, as he scattered and collected the fruits of other people's labor.   He had never rebelled or protested his inheritance of fully loaded wheeling and dealing genes.   And why should he?—his genes fit him perfectly for the life he led. In fact had seen him comfortably through events of sufficient trauma that would have leveled anyone less genetically endowed—the marriages, divorces, children—the dismantling and rebuilding of his empire, all had seemed pre-ordained to spin out with little sweat to him. So the legacy had been easy for him to accept.

His donors were proud, too. They had been proud, when even as a child his obstreperous behavior required that they call in reinforcement nurses and nannies, because they knew in their heart of hearts, that his staying power against all suggestions of temperance, signaled the kind of leadership qualities the world awaited. But now there was this baffling shift that had begun an unsettling raid on the balance sheet of his life.

Strangely, at some level, there was an intense longing to find something totally foreign to his previous experiences, yet had a familiar tugging at some vital parts that made him increasingly anxious.

He wondered if there had been a slight leak in his gene pool that allowed this foreign matter to seep into his psyche and over the years spread to a pocket of his mind where it had begun to drip, drip, drip, an arresting, intermittent, drumming of droplets on his conscious being. He sensed that his current set up was decidedly impure. He wondered if his rambunctious genes had not allowed him the experience of purity—had in fact robbed him of innocence and left him bereft of the one thing money and power couldn't buy—dignity, the most highly regarded calling of the day. He was sure that a truly immaculate strain of innocence would be so strong and pure that it could not be permeated—set up for acquisition, merger, or take over— the methods for success with which he was familiar. He must find the original source somewhere within him and cultivate it— nurture it—sacrifice for it, or dignity would never be his.

The piercing pain of loneliness

He wondered if this slight crack with the uncharacteristic substance suddenly afloat, was a sign that there still was a path to glory.

Toward that goal, he would travel those roads he had rejected—consume simple country cooking with gravy over everything—explore the hopes and dreams— experienced in scaled down pleasure palaces. He would stay in cheap motels— lie on a bed and watch the sign with missing bulbs in the first letter, blink out its invitation— lotel—lotel—lotel. He would drink from pure white Styrofoam cups, eager to please, but sadly disposable—fill sorry plastic ice buckets from a coin machine down the hall—no room service, no demands, no interruptions— no more cumbersome, conspicuous consumption, hanging around his neck like a heavy gold chain of incredible folly, that dragged him down.   The stark bareness posed as a kind of honesty. It was, what it was— no pretensions allowed.

He would sit on a bench in the park of a town square and listen to the local band's exquisite rendition of the Stars and Stripes Forever. He would ask that the innocence of the flaws in the band shell and the rendition spill their imperfections over him in absolution. (though at his level of recognition he felt no evidence of having committed harmful transgressions, but still—). He would prostrate himself on the ground and examine every, dew kissed, blade of grass and beg to be anointed by their perfection. He wanted to feel his life—touch it with this tentative feeling of sensitivity— hold it close, then offer it up like a chalis to receive the purity and innocence that would surely dribble down from the recently activated corner of his gene pool—if he stayed the course.

And lastly, he would sit in an all night diner, enveloped in ominous lighting, experiencing the piercing pain of loneliness that he had never been permitted to endure. He was not sure why this vision called to him, filled him with melancholy, and left him on the verge of tears.

All of this new found path to glory he would share with his precious companion, whom he saw in a completely different light with a different role to play. He would show his appreciation for the candor with which she described the Dichotomy painting for his benefit. This selfless act he knew would surely bring gross ridicule on her otherwise kind and gentle demeanor. He now believed she was simply masquerading as a vixen, to cover up her incredulous desire to please. What else could he expect from one so perfectly constructed, amply affectionate, and freshly concocted from her gene reservoir of Pablum and floating talcum powder?

She surely would not fleece his wallet, pry promises out of him, or try to force him to reprise the role he suddenly and passionately wished to leave behind. He rejoiced in the brave dialogue of the Barbie's perception of the Dichotomy, springing from a mouth so deliciously round and juicy, with just the teeniest tremor of a lisp—so innocent and childlike, that the itty-bitty tuck in the corner of her mouth, like a retention basin picking up the slack on the baby drool, permitted the soft quaking, slurping, voice, to breathlessly speak those innocent naughty words. The embodiment of this infantile purity, he deemed to be an affirmation of his quest for an idyllic transformation. He knew in time she would exult in the simple, raw, unvarnished, dreary, pristine path of his odyssey. In fact, his hurtling elements would surely jump start her own search for a prime, polished, life nugget of the rarest kind. This is the way he would live as soon as this latest deal—last deal, was consummated. The change was important to his survival.

He caught a buzz that reached all the way to his fingertips—not a power jolt, like he was accustomed to, but a click to reset his timer for longer, slower, days and nights in which to find the missing pieces of the puzzle of his life.

All of these scenes and emotions swirled around in his head, making him woozy and his gait unsteady, as the gallery patrons crowded around for the chance to shake his hand, or at least catch a nod of his head in some real or imagined cause for kinship.

For Barbie's part, she was proud that her sexually explicit reading of the tedious, melodramatic composition, Dichotomy, had deeply affected the mogul. In fact her reading reinforced a growing awareness that it was something she did well—a skill so sly it was hard to define or recognize. Everyone was born with a talent for survival and she had found hers and would continue to develop and polish it to meet further challenges. She knew that her public deconstruction of the heralded center piece of Laura's Art Show was a powerful coup in itself—in fact, the fit of complex logistics turned out to be a new and disarming addition to her accumulating talents.

She knew what the painting was all about—the struggle for equality in a changing world. But this persistent quandary would not be resolved in her life time and she saw herself as an old fashioned girl, with an up-tempo beat, willing to let the painter lady do the heavy lifting, until she wore herself out—became old and frumpy, wore caftans and sandals—long stringy hair and no makeup.

No doubt the artist would continue to paint her moody, gender equality musings—present them to the passing throngs—

currently shielding their newly, cautious, deaf eyes—ignoring the accomplishments of the trailblazers who trampled the weeds of opposition at great personal sacrifice to attain the choices currently available. But now they marched along the paths smoothed out for them and only occasionally glanced back over their flawless shoulders, with curiosity and disdain for the artist's cumbersome, outmoded attitudes. They would sport their tucked and tightened bodies—burgeoning boobs—nipped noses—enhanced eyes—and other assorted adjustments to snare a suitable meal ticket, the tried and true traditional way. Money the great equalizer.   This was how the real gender balance worked.

And this Barbie would stay young and cute forever. The Lamp would see to it no matter where he was, she saw that in his needy aging eyes. In fact she saw something oddly out of place for a man of his stature and reputation. She was surprised at how easy it had been to snag him and wondered what it was he saw that set her apart. There were always those hoards of attractive and aggressive young women trying to trap him in any way possible.   She   thought   he   had   recently   become uncharacteristically vulnerable in some vaguely, concealed area. She sensed a distinct change in attitude, that threw her highly trained animal instincts on high alert. She must protect her prey, lest the pack catch the scent and attempt a raid. She would have to shepherd him through the crowds, using the best of her genes which had been passed down to her as almost perfect head to toe body parts and the motorized accessories to operate them to her advantage.

Like the mogul, she too was pleased with her endowments. They had taken her out of a dead end existence in a dead end little town where watching the paint dry was an animated activity. The expressways had left it behind to die of boredom. She had nearly suffocated there. The stultifying discussions of her young, married friends as to the benefits of cloth diapers over disposable—which was better for the health of the child and protection of the environment, felt like a strangle hold on her throat. They seemed smug in their small world cocoons, combining the best of the new with the tried and true of the old, to keep their corner of the universe neat and tidy. Sturdy stock— secure, fearless and capable of leaping tall buildings in a single bound, if called upon to do so. These were the super caretakers—animal and tree snugglers—custodians of the unwritten rules of respect and dignity for flora and fauna— ecological, maintenance people testing the wind and water and finding it to their liking.

But fortunately the Barbie's glorious, body perfect, genes had catapulted her out of this debilitating fairground via the beauty pageants, to the big city—the big deals—the big people, and the big money. It would have been stupid for someone of her perfectness not to give pleasure to a greater audience and finally a select few. In fact it would be a terrible waste. And of all the things she might be accused of, wasting her natural resources, would not be one of them. In any case, it had all been preordained. But now she needed to get the top ticket's wavering attention, and steer him out of the clinging crowd.

The Relationship, shaken by a spasm of indecision, wanted to accompany the beautiful Laura back to her studio of colorful, reflections of life, or even to follow Harold on his trek to locate Honey—to hear him speak the words that had finally been loosened from his tightly clenched brain—Love and Commitment.

But they had all dumped it, like a bag of trash. A lump was forming in its throat as the humiliation crept up the back of its neck and flushed its face, but was soon followed by the resolve to get even. It needed to get back on its track to fame and fortune and so quickly switched its limited allegiance to the stellar couple and was rewarded with a curt directive from the suddenly transformed, Sergeant Barbie, instructing it to haul butt and help her escort the grinning vacancy, registered on the face of the staggering mogul —out to a slap of cold night air.

A slap of a different kind was delivered via the tabloid headline the following week. "Powerful Little Pinky Takes Center Stage" it blasted. The accompanying photo showed the Dichotomy painting—Barbie's tiny little pinky finger stuck in the Titan's mouth—and in the background, Charlie in shock mode, the Relationship's eyes popping in horror—little fingers splayed across its open mouth and a galvanized assortment of gallery gapers.

The caption read, "Dirty Picture Stuns Art World." The Barbie had usurped the artist's throne temporarily, with her small poisoned dart—stolen the thunder from the attending pompous and great pretenders—the faux this and that's—the con artists— stealing bits and pieces of other people's lives to make themselves acceptable—and leveled the playing field with slime. But she had proved her point—this truly was the current way the real gender balance worked. Still, it was a hallow victory of sorts, for deep in her heart of hearts—given the options, she would rather have been Laura.

The Art World responded with a grand pout, by dimming their gallery lights for a week and mourning the incivility creeping into their ranks. The publicity brought an unprecedented avalanche of attention on the Dichotomy, which was heralded as the most important work of the decade. The painting, resting comfortably, in Laura's lake house, after its tumultuous ride, had ultimately raised the level of discourse on the equality of women's roles, where the subject had been waning The artist occasionally paused in front of the canvas, her Mona Lisa smile flickering into soft laughter, as she contemplated the paradox of the unfortunate, Barbie's bimbo, eruption, becoming the catalyst for restarting the inquiry into how best to keep the disproportional seesaw of life engrossing, but with equal though different weight on each side. In the end, Dichotomy, had been the appropriate title.

The Relationship, sickened by the gross publicity, hoped, at least, that it had landed on the right side of the fall-out and could take advantage of the fracas to gain ground in its quest for fame and fortune on the Talk Shows.

And so, in the months that followed, lived with the duo— traveled with them—and stole their secrets. It watched and listened and noted that this couple never touched anything with tenderness—not even each other. Not the way Honey tapped everything with love. But that was not pertinent to the business at hand. The important thing was, not to lose sight of its goals to reach stardom, while help was still at hand. And so it paid close attention to the art of the deal and how to press for favors.

Eventually, the Relationship learned to mimic the moves, the speech, and characteristics of its mentor. Its mentor, however, fraught with intermittent concentration on serious negotiations—was increasingly slipping into dream sequences, aided and abetted by Norman Rockwell prints, inserted between position papers. But what worried the Relationship most of all was the recurring painting of "Nighthawks," by the artist Edward Hopper. There were copies of this eerie, nocturnal, scene, imbued with the stark loneliness of an all night diner—

placed in desk drawers, file cabinets, on walls, and inside his coat room door.

Frequently, the grand titan projected himself into the painting—adopting the punishing hurt he saw in the lonely diner. He began wearing a forties fedora and tattered suit coat like the one worn by the solitary customer seated at the counter. He had traded an Armani suit for the trappings of a street derelict and felt cheap about the exchange; believing he had compromised the man in the deal to pursue his own goal—a habit he found hard to break. Still, the awareness of the breach, was in itself a hopeful sign in his new carnation—one in which he realized at once that of the two men, he was the true derelict. He believed the pain searing suffering of isolation in the diner might be offered up to coax his elusive, sapling gene, to release the source of original innocence, he felt sure was there. He wished to be dispossessed of the comforts inherited from both parents, which had been the center of his life, and reach back to the unknown substance. He held fast to the thick coffee mug in hopes the vibrations of a sudden thunder clap would loosen the stubborn particulate matter in his head and release the cumulative deposits—in the form of cleansing rain. This source would be his only route to dignity—the purity to restart his life's journey. He must maintain his vigil.

The Relationship thought this whole hike in the woodlands would end in a pile of diddly squat and was growing weary of this flaky connection. It had accompanied Larry the Lamp on part of his road trip, absent the Dolly, but now the time was ripe to profit from the collected scoop it needed to score and it was afraid that their weirdness would rub off on it.   It hardly recognized the Barbie anymore, she spent so much time at spas and body shops—foreign and domestic. And the last time it saw its mentor, he appeared to have taken up permanent residence in the soul snatching nocturnal light of the all night diner—waiting for his epiphany.

The Relationship was weary of the mogul's groveling around, looking for some "goody-two-shoes" gene that may have slipped from the drainage of a wussy relative. And it was revolted by the eerie, green reflection of the florescent light that laid on the lonely Lamp's cold, black coffee, like an oil slick on an asphalt street puddle.   It was time to turn the bag of tricks, chits and credits, it had collected into the big blast of its special little life. The world needed to know their famous creation was about to kick butt. And so at last it split from the hoi polloi, to ply its trade for the big bang it always wanted—its ego craved— more than anything—crash into the scene of the ratings busting TV Talk Shows and pull the audience out of their seats and into its gritty little fan club— from which it would skyrocket into its own show.   Then it would have the power to influence and control—to be feared—sought after—listened to—revered?— Why not? This was the ultimate—the height of heights—the pinnacle.   The possibilities and prospects sucked on the Relationship's brain again, leaving it light headed with incomparable visions. The World's Most Famous Relationship would interview other Relationships of the rich and famous—infamous—notorious—nefarious—even the little Sigh Abuse Relationship would have its day in court. The tell all sequences would reveal untold sludge and mire that only real Relationships could know. The unvarnished, unmitigated down and dirty—from inside the boardroom and under the bed—with tapes and pictures. But first it would have to try its wings—get exposure.

And so in time, it selected the Talk Show that had the highest ratings and the most well known ring master and dragged its bag of lumps and rocks to sling at random.

Showdown at the Talk Show Corral

As the cameras panned around the room and settled on the Talk Show Host/Personality, the studio audience appeared to be in a receptive mood. A warm and welcoming, round of applause greeted her. Seated on the stage of the Greatest Show on Earth, its small frame nearly lost in the guest chair, the Relationship rested its right foot on its left knee—posing a relaxed yet commanding demeanor. It smiled and grinned, turning from side to side reflecting in its long sought after High Self Esteem, which beamed out from every make-up polished pore— frequently nodding its head in the televangelical mode of affirmation of its elevated state—a move it had found immensely disarming in doing deals.

With the licorice lollipop microphone close to her mouth, the talk show host said, "I'm sure you are all aware of the frequency with which we have featured discussions about relationships on this show—relationships of all shapes and sizes—with all degrees of pain and complications—from all walks of life. And so today, let us welcome The World's Most Famous Relationship." There was a smattering of applause. "And so, tell us how you arrived at this celebrity status." It was her style to begin every sentence with "And so."

The Relationship pushed out its round, plump lips into a round, plump circle, then pulled them back, cracking an insipid smile. It spread its hands wide apart—palms up, in another ministerial move toward sanctity, but strangely, it stopped short of receiving blessings, and made a crude attempt at humor.

"Let's just say—humility was not my Trump card. Get it, Trump card?" The pious demeanor and the silly remark did not fit. It caught the audience off guard and startled the Relationship. Its timing was off. How could it screw up like this? It would have to go for damage control—steer the conversation out of this path and back on the star track. It had probably weakened its pathetic rags to riches testimonial, but that could be patched up. Still, it would have to pay closer attention and watch its motor driven mouth. But what was that she was saying?

"It's been said, in fact, that you took advantage of people who put their trust in you."

Something was definitely wrong here. Was this the part in the host's screwdriver, interview technique, where people let down their guard and began to unravel? That couldn't happen. This was the one and only chance to play all of its roles— execute the perfect performance, at this all important audition for a Talk Show of its own.

The Relationship leaned forward bracing its hands on the arms of the chair. A distraction would turn things around. It would try to slip in another slice of humor. "Trust, whoa! What's with this trust gig? Is this a talk show or a game show? What are we playing here, Who Can You Trust?" It cracked another simpy grin and cackled. Splat! The Doyenne of Day Time was in a drilling mode.

"And so, is it not true that you manipulated friends that trusted you? That in your quest for success you ran over innocent people and railroaded others, that you weaseled information from? And were you not responsible for the split up of the couple that trusted you and made you, The World's Most Famous Relationship?" Her voice was winging way up—like a prosecuting attorney, as she walked up and down, sucking on that stupid licorice microphone. The Relationship knew it was too late to throw in that Larry the Lamp had left the real world, on his own recognizance, and was now ensconced in his pew at the all night diner, and having taken the clothes and the place from the Nighthawk guy, was maintaining the stake-out for his epiphany—And more importantly that it had accompanied the mogul on his Odyssey, in fact had become his enabler—even as the ever resourceful, Barbie, was being sculptured one more time, while planning yet another end run on a vulnerable, fading, star with weighty money bags dragging him down to a slow scamper. This was all wrong. It had been a truly helpful Relationship, reliable, trustworthy, loyal. Their split was not its fault. This was not fair.

"What do you think, audience?" She moved up to a guy in about the third row and thrust the black lollipop in his face. "Yes, sir, what is your comment?"

"I think this Relationship is a scumbag—a real dirt ball. It's all the creepy things that drive people apart. You can't have a love affair anymore, you have to have a crummy Relationship in there screwing up the works—sticking its face in where it doesn't belong. I'll never trust a Relationship again."

"Wait a minute—wait a minute," shouted the Relationship. "You want to talk about trust? I'll tell you who I trust. I trust the bottom line, that's what I trust," it said in a mogul mouth incantation. "The bottom line is the Word."

"Your bottom line, right? And so, what about the friends and associates you conned out of their bottom lines—their life dreams and self worth?"

"Self worth, you say," said the Relationship, feigning hurt feelings "What about my self worth?" This seemed like the perfect time to sing the accused criminal number—that was always effective—play on those guilt and pity strings.

"Hey, gimme a break. I suffer from Low Self Esteem. I've been smacked around like a hockey puck from one team to another. Nobody ever cared about me, or ever wanted me—for long," whined the Relationship. It forgot to mention the dysfunctional family bit.

"Who would want you, you destructive little twit?" someone hollered out. The talk show diva hurried over to the woman, flipping the microphone, in a flashy wrist movement, from lips to lips—"You wanted to say what?"—to the talker.

"I said who would want a repulsive little destroyer like that living with them? I've been trying to get rid of a manipulative Relationship just like that for years."

The Relationship was hurt and disappointed at the way its day of days was turning out. That wicked talk show woman had made a shambles of its dream. Anger was beginning to surge through its body and out of its mouth—bypassing the control valve of its brain. "Put your head around this, Tinker Bell. You seem to forget, I'm sitting on a bunch of power, here. I know where the bodies are buried—big bodies—important bodies," it shouted. Where did that come from? It sounded like a hit man. Turn it around. Put it back in her court. Stay on point.

The Relationship's adrenal glands went on full alert. "You want to talk about trust and bottom lines? You're nothing but an over paid carnival barker for the Greatest Freak Show on Earth. You drag the dregs of humanity out here and let the voyeurs of the world titter and cluck. You spur your studio audience to cast disparaging remarks, cruel comments, and demeaning insinuations on your so-called guests. Guests, geez, you hammer them down until they are so ashamed and embarrassed that they go home to hide in a closet for the rest of their lives. Talk about a con. You get your guests to spill their guts to fill your coffers. What an altruistic fraud you are. You hypo—hippo hippo crate"—oh no not the weight thing. "Get real—your bottom line isn't all that clean and smooth, Sister Mary Wonderful."

Ignoring this negative delivery, the talk show person said, "And so, again, is it not true that you caused the split of the couple who trusted you and made you the World's Most Famous Relationship?" There were catcalls, whistles, and boos from the studio audience—and then a sudden whooshing of air smacked upside its head. Good grief, was it being attacked by the sigh abuse faction described by the Married Relationship on the beach?

It had been hit broadside by a powerful cross current. How could it have missed the signs—the chalk arrows on the pavement—the bread crumbs in the forest? It should have known a giant sea change was coming when its mentor, Larry the Lamp, abruptly sprinted for the tall grass. What had happened to the flashy, greedy icons that everybody worshipped—tried to emulate? Had they all wussed out—possibly been inflicted by an epidemic of Harolditis? Who cared, it wasn't going to take this unwarranted abuse lying down. It would give as good as it got. There was still time to get the just desserts it so richly deserved Down and dirty—filthy and obscene, that was the ticket to the high stakes game. Always was, always would be—never mind the closets, they had all been cleaned out and put up for auction—pull up the rug and show what's underneath. The Relationship turned its ire on the talk show driller.

"What about you, you opportunistic chameleon, you work both sides of the street turning green for the dollars and brown for the crud you spread. You send your troops out to dredge up the pond scum. You're nothing but a bottom feeler" Bottom feeler? Oh geez, the word is feeder—bottom feeder. " Then you primp around and expose any needy soul willing to prostitute itself for that all important fifteen minutes of shame." Shame? Close, but no cigar. And what about primp? Never mind, keep up the momentum—"Did you think you could turn this sow's purse into a silk ear?" Nothing was working. It couldn't even swear effectively. What were the real words—the dirty words? It seemed to have lapsed into Honey mouth—with her dyspeptic pattern of speech. Its timing was way off. The entire world's timing was off. Somebody had changed the program. While it was running so hard for the gold, they had moved the signs and spoiled its chances for success. The whole thing was a set up. Damn that talking twister of fate. When did this, Perry Mason, in drag begin to adopt the epiphany in her own personal market place?

The audience began to make strange thumping and chanting noises, that sounded like Woof—Woof—Woof. They were out of control. The Relationship sensed some frightening vibes. It thought it saw some uniformed security guards coming toward the stage. Quickly, it pulled the clip-on microphone from its collar, ran down the steps and up the center aisle between the crazed masses—its little feet slapping the floor as it ran. Reaching the exit door of the studio, the Relationship turned around and hollered,

"A fox on all your houses." Then it sped out into the hallway and down the main staircase. It was frightened, but its brain kicked in again and plans began to form. It would go home to Honey. She would take it back. Throw her a few crumbs—a hard luck story and voila—a place to rest and start over.

Its heart was pounding from terror and exertion as it reached the public phone area in the lobby. Hopping up on the attached seat of a booth, it dropped a coin in the slot and tapped out Honey's number. She would be there—she would give it another chance. One ring—two—three—where the heck was she?—four, oh my God—five—click—click. Ah merciful heavens. The answering machine at the other end said, "Hi, this is Honey—I'm far away from the phone right now. I know you're out there, Harold. Listen up or you'll be late for life. Do you hear all those voices, Harold? No, of course you don't. The air is clear of all mouth pollution. There is only one voice, and it's mine. I've learned to trust myself. I found the missing piece of the puzzle. It's me. You know where to find me, Harold. I'm at the Castle with Running Water in Every Room. The Relationship is gone, Harold—down the tubes—bye bye— finito—outta here. Its Geography."

You got a Limo?

The Relationship dropped the phone, slipped to the floor, sank to its knees and began to sob. The instrument swung back and forth, repeating the last part of the recorded message—"its geography—its geography—its geography." Leave it to Honey to screw up its final scene.

So, at last it was over. The trip to Valhalla had come to a screeching halt, due to inclement behavior. There would be no more last minute reprieves. It was the end of an era. There would be a new and different kind of hero in the future, endowed with the ability to count past Number One, and the fortitude to plug into the courage connection. Harold would make a difference with his quirky, best selling book, "Treasures in the Attic of Your Mind" Harold, the dream writer, with his disdain for coins and anything monetary, had pulled it off, finally, big time, and in the same fashion as the Breath Mint commercial. His sappy serious pledge to save the children had struck a resounding chord and captured the speed driven souls, causing them to slow down and open up the attics of their minds. And the frenzied acceptance of the book along with the amulets of human preservation (now being sold as a package) caused tons of dirty coins to rain down upon Harold's flabbergasted head.

And Honey's program of "Same Time-Different Places," in which schools and businesses began and ended at the same hour, removed the need for Day Care Centers. Compressing hours and eliminating useless, wasteful, habits and rituals would allow all work to be accomplished in half the time. Her curious methods, complete with a warehouse of collectible slogans and captivating jingles—presented the type of cooperative effort long sought after by parents, but never before articulated in such simple, easy to follow directions. With Honey's words put to the plan, it became an instant phenom.

Concentrate—maintain your focus
Don't waste thoughts on hocus pocus
When your chores are left behind
You will have your own Dream Time.

So much had changed—the Relationship had not only missed the handwriting on the wall, but the paint on the canvas, as Laura's spunky little ironing board, having made it up from the basement and out of the laundry room, became the interior decorator's cause celeb—dressed in lace and ruffled skirts to the floor—over feet of brass balls, for the drawing room—that plainly said, "Don't mess with the dress." And tailored suits for the boardroom—the legs ending in dainty, satin slippers, announcing, "Walk softly while wearing a big suit."

The boards traveled—went on vacations —appeared at political rallies done up in party bunting and frequently used as a podium—eventually they were recognized as natural motivators, where the mesmerizing stroking of iron on therapeutic fiber was said to imbue the mind with ideas of incomparable quality. And when ideas, planning and execution failed to produce a satisfactory result, creative people were often heard to say, "Well, back to the ironing board."

So what, so what, so what!

So what if it picked the wrong pony and spent itself on the hocus pocus. Who cared? The Relationship was interested in preserving its heritage. It wanted to take its place in history along with all of the other pop culture idols—the "Me" people—the "Power Brokers," and the "Heart Breakers," that were part of the scene where fame and fortunes were grabbed and lost, and love affairs were shattered . Its star was fading, but no one would ever forget the significance of its name, "Relationship."

Someone would write a best selling book about the sadness of its quest to belong—to be loved, warts and all—to be dumped and still persevere—its scrape with the fickle fate of timing—and sell the movie rights. All the details of its struggle to achieve fame and fortune would be revealed—its misconceptions and misplaced loyalties and especially the miraculous last minute sleight of hand that plucked it from the jaws of the salivating masses and kept its wandering piece of the puzzle in play.

The Relationship made a pathetic squeak from its position on the floor. A stranger seeing the phone dangling—squawking its final message and the prostrate body of the Relationship on the floor—bent over the tiny figure and placed his ear near the round, tear stained, kissey face, world famous pucker, and asked, "Are you all right? Can I help you?"

"I want to go home," said the tiny voice from down under."

"And where might that be?" asked the stranger.

"To the castle with running Water in Every Room," said the Relationship, breathing a sigh of relief—snuggling up, all warm and cuddly—open—innocent— trusting—caring. This was the way it always began.

"You know how to get there?" asked the stranger.

"You got a limo?" said the endearing little creature.

About The Author

Joyce Payne is a writer whose work has frequently appeared in the Chicago Sunday Tribune. An advertising copywriter with national accounts, she received the annual award from the Mail Advertising Club of Chicago. Through a series of newspaper columns, the Relationship made its first appearance and began a life of its own.

Mother of four grown children, Joyce, currently resides with her husband and dogs atop a high ridge overlooking vast mountain ranges and valleys, where the coyotes howl and the wind blows free.